Mississippi Whispers

Alexis Heflin

To
Lucy
Thanks for your
Support
Love Alexis

Quantity discounts are available on bulk orders. Contact
sales@TAGPublishers.com for more information.

TAG Publishing, LLC
2030 S. Milam
Amarillo, TX 79109
www.TAGPublishers.com
Office (806) 373-0114
Fax (806) 373-4004
info@TAGPublishers.com

ISBN: 978-1-59930-432-8

Editors: Valerie Leary and Teresa Leary McLendon

First Edition

Dedication

For my two sons, John and Rick; my granddaughter Emily Ann; my brothers and sisters, Margie, Lena, Leon; and Gene, Willie F, and Ray, who have passed; my nieces and nephews; and the friends too numerous to name who have supported and encouraged me to tell the story of Buddy Heflin.

Contents

Alexis Heflin

Foreword
Summer 2013
By Valerie Leary

The troubled history of Mississippi is well-known. The state has had its share of dark secrets and prejudice and crime. The harsh realities of Mississippi's past affect the people of Mississippi, and this fact reveals itself in strong emotion portrayed in song, film, photography and legend rife with political implications. The destructive, dark times in Mississippi are the result of powerful people who abuse and hurt because they lack understanding of the gift and responsibility that comes with authority. They become feared but never respected. To try to understand, one can contemplate the truth and beauty of the Mississippi landscape. The Mississippi River winds across and down the country and continues where the waters are warm, fresh and deep. Translated, "Mississippi" means "great river." As blood feeds flesh, this river gives life to the land. These swamp environments are primal and wild, yet simple and safe because Nature follows fearful but sensible rules.

Nature does not have to be taught the difference between right and wrong; Nature does not blur the lines between necessity and greed. The fierce alligators of the Mississippi Delta thrive as do their prey. So, unlike powerful people, alligators are not only to be feared, but they are to be respected. The light of the moon illuminates the eyes of the alligators hidden in the mud, and then the ground begins to move with strength and purpose. The reptile returns to the depths of the swamp with what it needs to survive. The massive root systems extend tangled in the dark water and remind us of our limits--what we do not know and cannot figure out. The laws of man are not the same as the laws of

Nature. Unlike Nature, mankind breaks the rules and what follows is the necessity to hide, threaten and keep secrets so that at times it becomes difficult for people entangled in the secrets to uncover the truth.

The man for whom this memoir is written was rumored to be murdered and thrown into the Mississippi River. His body has never been found, nor was there ever a proper investigation, but that in no way means that his mysterious disappearance will sink to the depths and be forgotten.

The alligators have inhabited the Delta Swamps and have swum in the brackish water where fresh water meets sea water for millions of years. These solitary territorial animals have seen humans only recently considering the date of the American Revolution, 1776. Fast forward a few years to 1812, and the British again fought the English settlers to seize New Orleans and the vast territory acquired with the Louisiana Purchase. General Andrew Jackson's troops defeated the British and, in recognition of his victory, Jackson became and continues to be the capital of Mississippi. With the 1830 Treaty of Dancing Rabbit, the Native Americans traded the Delta land with the white settlers for land in Oklahoma.

The Delta Plantations that came after were larger than life all due to the fertile soil, so good for growing cotton. Clarksdale, Mississippi, was known as "The Golden Buckle on the Cotton Belt," but as charming as this image is, we know that only through the exploitation of African-American laborers were the Delta Plantations able to flourish. There are few antebellum structures left standing in Jackson because the Union forces captured the city of Jackson during the American Civil War (1841-1845) and destroyed most of them in an attempt to destroy the chains of slavery. Still, as Martin Luther King, Jr. emphasized in his "I Have A Dream" speech, "one hundred years later," in 1962 we witness the capital city placed under martial law by the order of Congress and President Kennedy as a result of riots by the Mississippi people refusing to allow James Meredith to attend classes at the University of Mississippi.

The person for whom this story has been written, my uncle, John Lloyd "Buddy" Heflin, was present on that day in 1962; he was a member of the Mississippi Army National Guard and among the troops called in to bolster law enforcement so that a young man who wanted to pursue his education could attend classes. My Aunt Alexis Heflin was at home pregnant with their first child while her husband spent two weeks on the college campus providing security for James Meredith.

William Faulkner once said, "To understand the world, you must first understand a place like Mississippi." Mississippi's haunted past raises the question of what could have been. If only…

Today the social and political tensions have changed, and Mississippi is famous for things other than segregation and its role in the Civil Rights Movement. There is the music, too — Gospel, Blues, and R&B. Artists as diverse as Charlie Daniels, Kid Rock, The Rolling Stones, and of course, Johnny and June have all written songs about the city of Jackson. One song in particular by June and Johnny Cash called "Jackson" is about newlyweds making the discovery that, after jumping much too quickly into marriage, the "fire" died out of their relationship. Buddy and Alexis got married in Starkville, Mississippi, not too far from Jackson, but the "fire" in their marriage was never the problem.

The problem in their marriage is a mystery and the reason for this book. John Lloyd "Buddy" Heflin was only twenty five when he disappeared. He was seen for the last time on December 31, 1968, in Jackson, Mississippi. Alexis Heflin married her first and only love, Buddy Heflin, and they had two sons. He vanished on New Year's Eve over forty years ago from Jackson, Mississippi, and no one in his family knows why or what happened to him.

My name is Valerie, and I never knew my uncle. I cannot remember not remembering my Aunt Lexi. Most of my aunts and uncles on both sides lived far away, but Aunt Lexi visited often. She would arrive, and the laughter would begin — infectious laughter about casual subjects that came up in conversation involving the whole family, sitting together in our small living room on chairs, the sofa and any space on the floor just to be close enough to Aunt Lexi to hear every word. No one wanted to miss the remark or recollection of a family memory that unexpectedly became hysterically funny. I am not completely sure about everyone else, but I can say that I fully believe that God blessed this family with the gift of being able to laugh uncontrollably at a family member's funeral. I will be flattered that my friends and family find the chance to laugh at mine — laughter through tears is one of my favorite emotions. I do not have any other explanation for this ability to crack up laughing, and I mean laugh-till-you-cry laughter, at the most ordinary of comments, but that is the way we are.

So, what you are about to read is something that I have taken on because of my life-long admiration for my aunt and my passion for reading words clearly inspired by an author's desire to tell the small part of their purpose in God's kingdom with words that are true, encouraging and forgiving.

Having said all of that, please remember that memory, although a priceless part of what shapes our lives, can be very convincing even when the facts want to argue. The legal documents themselves that we obtained to double check dates and names have errors. The care taken to accurately tell the story is considerable. This is Alexis Heflin's story as told to my sister and me, and then written by me in her voice, first person.

My part in writing this book for my aunt came about quite suddenly three years after she had already gathered the documents, organized her thoughts and collaborated with different people on the 3000 words that were in my hands. People cannot help but be drawn to my aunt because she is personable, funny, strong and so compassionate. Curious about her northern accent and how she came to be in Huntsville, Alexis eventually answered enough questions and heard enough times that she needed to write her story down on paper.

That initial read told me that the next-to-impossible part of getting a novel started had been done, but the words were not my Aunt Lexi's voice. My sister was the first to see it. I was assigned the task because I am the English major in the family; I have taught Language Arts for over twenty years. Aunt Lexi tells the story while I write.

My aunt lived in Obion, Tennessee, until her mother, Callie Hamilton, died unexpectedly in the winter of 1946. My aunt was three years old, and her father, a gentle, God-fearing man, moved his family back to his hometown of Clarksdale, Mississippi, to keep all seven of his children under one roof. He intended to farm to provide for his children, and he bought a house for the family on Mr. Posey's *plantation where he and my aunt's older brothers worked the fields. Back in Obion, where all seven children were born, their mother's family had discussed separating the children. That is how it was done back then. With no mother people assumed the father could not handle the seven children, but Cas Hamilton (1903-1974) did and never remarried. Each child attended Walnut School, grew up, got married and moved on. After graduating from high school, my aunt married Buddy Heflin (1961), and within seven years (1968) he vanished without a trace.*

Alexis Heflin wants to tell her story as a tribute to this man who was full of love, devotion, humor, compassion, dreams, and yes, faults. She has been writing this story for forty years, while the summers and winters come and go, and come again. Time to move on? Let go? How do you do that, really? There are thousands of unsolved cases of loved ones' mysterious disappearances which means that there are thousands of broken-hearted people who will never fully be able to rest without the knowledge of what really happened to the loved one they lost without a trace. My aunt, unfortunately, is not alone in this experience.

After he disappeared, my aunt and her two boys were left to fend for themselves, but she did have the help of family, friends, and prayers. The three of them were able to stay together as a family; she had learned how to do that from her father; but the lesson she learned by his example did not make it any less difficult. Her children waited for their daddy to come home as she waited to find out what happened to him. She knows that Buddy would have come home to his boys if he could have. He was a devoted father, and even though they were still so young, both Johnny and Ricky remember that bond. Could he have made bad decisions and been mixed up with people involved in criminal activity in their small town? Probably. But did he choose to leave his life without a trace or a word to his family? Absolutely not.

As a result of new evidence and Aunt Lexi's determination to find the truth for her sons, in October of 2010 the Mississippi Bureau of Investigations reopened this forty-one-year-old cold case. Forty years ago she had known from the police and witnesses that her husband's car was found at a truck stop riddled with bullet holes and blood. She had heard rumors that her husband's body had been thrown into the Mississippi River after he was murdered by experienced and well-known criminals. The police, however, deemed it necessary to end the investigation due to lack of evidence. Is it any wonder that she has questioned their motives in that decision all of these years? In any case, she had no answers.

But Alexis Heflin still has hope that her boys and she will finally have closure. So many people who knew Buddy Heflin have begun to come forward with their stories, and she has been in contact with investigators in Mississippi who promise to do all they can to find out the truth. She knew she would one day write the story, but she is less sure about the ending. She would like to have the story told so that people who read it might come forward with information. Time goes on, and it gets less and less likely that anyone will admit responsibility. The memories of possible witnesses to Buddy Heflin's murder or his decision to "disappear," have surely grown dimmer. People have moved away or perhaps convinced themselves not to get involved if they do know something about the case. Or, they have died and taken what they know to their graves. These thoughts have haunted my aunt off and on all these years. But now, she would like to lay Buddy Heflin and this agonizing reality to rest with a push *for help from the authorities and any remaining witnesses willing to come forward.*

In April of 2013, my aunt and I drove to Starkville, Mississippi, and met with three men who renewed her hope and have gained our complete confidence. We had the privilege of meeting with these FBI agents, and since then, there have been returned phone calls not to mention the DNA and lie detector tests following. Our family teaches that police officers are community members to trust, respect and rely upon for help, and we find that to be consistent with the agents in Mississippi who are in charge of the investigation now.

Part I:

Unexpected

and

Unexplained

CHAPTER 1
1960
Meeting Buddy Heflin

I MET BUDDY HEFLIN for the first time waiting tables at Thompson's Restaurant in 1960. Sparks flew, but how could I have guessed that I had just seen my future husband—a chance encounter that gave me my two cherished sons, a beautiful and gifted granddaughter, and a life spent searching for answers to what happened to Buddy Heflin. Coincidentally, the Andy Griffith Show aired for the first time in 1960, and on the surface, our town was not much different than Mayberry. We knew our neighbors, and they knew us. We were not unaware, however, that we were living in troubled times fraught with prejudice and criminal activity. Both could be avoided by choice, and my father made it clear that his children were to stay on the straight and narrow path. Thankfully, the Hamilton children had reputations that mirrored my father's teachings. Mrs. Thompson, who owned the local family restaurant, smiled and gave me a big hug as she assured, "Of course you can work for us Miss Hamilton."

Mr. and Mrs. Howard Thompson served the freshest vegetables, the best catfish and smoked barbeque, and people from miles around were regulars. During lunch, the students from Mississippi State University came to eat. Every day was packed, so I made very good tips. I was grateful for the work and looked forward to fulfilling my life-long dream of becoming a wife and mother.

I achieved my high-school diploma and found a steady job as a waitress. The next step was to find a husband, begin a family of my own and create a happy home with our own birthday celebrations and holiday traditions.

While working at the restaurant one day, my friend and fellow waitress Francis leaned over to me and said, "Look at that cute guy over by the pinball machine." Francis and I had gotten to know many customers by name, and the young men were all well-mannered and nicely dressed. But, neither of us had ever noticed this one. I looked over and saw the most handsome man I had ever seen. He was around my age with dark hair and skin and the most beautiful smile. He was so friendly with everyone, and it showed that he enjoyed his friends and having a good time. Francis saw him first and wanted to go over and talk to him, but she was too shy to go alone. That was what I was thinking at the time. In fact, she had already seen him looking at me. In fact, most everyone at the restaurant already knew he liked me.

She asked me to go with her. I had no idea what I was going to say, but nevertheless, we walked over to the pinball machine, and Francis stood behind me. Trying to be friendly I declared, "I have never played pinball before." I intended to start an easy conversation so that Francis could join in. We introduced ourselves, and he said his name was John. Buddy, his nickname, was really focused on the game he was playing, but he managed to talk with everyone standing around so that no one felt left out but very welcome.

It did not take me long to understand why he had the nickname of "Buddy." The group stayed together while he played about fifteen minutes more. He said that he needed to go, but he would be back another time. He looked at me when he said this, but I had only been looking at him the whole time. When his eyes caught mine, I smiled and sighed, "Okay. Bye." I wanted to say something else, but I was now the one who was being shy.

He did come back again and again, always playing pinball after he ate. His clothes were always neat and clean, and he was so polite and well-mannered. One day he came in and asked Francis and me if we wanted to go to another place to get a bite to eat at a diner down the road that played music and where the crowd was more our own ages. Buddy was waiting outside for us, and as we walked toward the car, he grabbed my hand and told me I could get in on his side of the car, and I did. We all piled in the front seat and went out to the diner, and we all had a great time that night. The next day I asked Francis if she were angry with me because I sat next to Buddy; I did not want her to think I was being pushy or had done it on purpose. I was not the kind of girl to steal a guy from a friend. I was so relieved when she said that she had seen him reach out and grab my hand, and she knew that I was the one he had his eye on. After that, everyone at the restaurant told me that they could see how much he fancied me and what a great-looking couple we were. Young couples moved at a slow pace back then, but I fell in love with Buddy from the moment I saw him. I eventually met two of Buddy's closest friends, Gail Wofford and Earl Burch. Gail and I are still in contact after all of these years. Sadly, Earl Burch took his own life shortly after Buddy's disappearance. I still wonder if there is a connection. Did Earl Burch choose suicide as a way to disconnect from the same trouble Buddy may have been in?

It was about a month later that Buddy asked me out on our first date to a nice steakhouse in town. I wanted to impress him and have everything go perfectly. He was so easy to be with. He would carry on and have everyone laughing and at ease, but I was still nervous. Buddy recalled and shared stories about his family and friends, and I began to talk about my family and friends. Both of us were and had good reason to be proud of our parents and siblings. I wore a periwinkle blue dress that came to my knees. I must have chosen the right dress because every now and then, he would pause and tell me how beautiful I was. After dinner he once again held my hand, but this time, I held his hand, too. Somehow holding his hand made me feel as if I had found my partner. My hand in his made me feel complete as my father had felt with my mother. This night was one of the most special nights of my life so far; I began to believe in the future. The evening ended with his walking to the door of my house and telling me what a great time he had. He went on to say that he could not wait until the next time I would go out with him. As the door closed behind me, I realized that I really liked him. I drifted off to sleep remembering the stories about his childhood and laughing.

As months passed, I knew I wanted to marry Buddy. I began to learn more about his life and family. He grew up in Starkville and had three sisters. His mom and dad were very proud of Buddy, and

I enjoyed the time we all spent together while I was dating Buddy. Sarah and Ike Heflin lived a simple life which revolved around their children, church and community. The world that Buddy knew growing up was worlds apart from the world of suspicions and fear that I fear he eventually met. Buddy's best friend Gail and his nephew Jimmy describe Buddy as extremely anxious, fearful and secretive in the months before he disappeared. Buddy's personality changed from the fun-loving, open and carefree character traits that had earned him the nickname of "Buddy" he had been known as since he was a child. His sisters were older and told stories about Buddy's childhood; they were fond of telling how excited they all were to have a little brother. Their family liked to laugh and tell jokes. Buddy liked school and sports, and on the weekends he frequented the skating rink. Buddy enjoyed his friends and never stopped making new ones. The 1960s in Mississippi were troubled times because organized crime rings were no secret. Buddy was reared by parents and raised in a community that made the effort to protect and teach, but who also fully understood the dangerous environment just beyond the skating rink.

He had been a good student and graduated from New Hope High School in Starkville, Mississippi. His sisters let me in on the fact that he was a better student before he started paying so much attention to girls. That did not surprise me. Buddy was so outgoing and friendly, and he reminded me of my older brothers in that way. Buddy's father owned the Phillips 66 station in Starkville, and Buddy worked there every day after school. After high school graduation, he proudly joined the Mississippi Army National Guard, and he took several courses at Mississippi State. He was still very young and not sure what he wanted to do, but he always worked very hard. He was ambitious and wanted to have a good life. When the work day was over, he socialized. His favorite pastimes were listening to good music and driving fast cars. Buddy was 19 years old when we met and 25 when he disappeared.

Once we starting dating, we went out together twice a week on both Friday and Saturday nights. We became regulars at the Southern Air Club on Highway 82 in Columbus. The club played great music from the 50s and 60s with live bands. Buddy and I were a couple, but there were plenty of single people our ages looking to find someone special. There was always a very large crowd which included some military men in uniforms. Buddy always looked so handsome in his National Guard uniform. Other girls definitely paid attention to him. We had been dating for nine months, and I could tell things were getting serious because we started talking about marriage and having children. Buddy and I were already an uncle and an aunt to our siblings' children, and we could not wait to start a family of our own.

Buddy picked me up one Saturday evening to go out to dinner. I wore my white sun-back dress that complemented the tan I had been working on. He had mentioned having a special night with just us, so we got dressed up and went to dinner instead of going to the club as usual. We sat down at the table that night at a seafood restaurant and ordered lobster, vegetables and a salad. I went to the ladies' room, and when I came back to the table, the waitress was standing very close to Buddy, whispering and smiling. Of course, I did not like this one bit, but all was forgotten when she returned with a dozen roses to give me from Buddy. I was very surprised to see the beautiful flowers. Then Buddy put a black box in front of me that he had tucked away in his pocket. He asked me to marry him. I was so happy, and, of course, I said, "Yes," and then opened the box and put on my engagement ring. I could not wait to start planning the wedding and become Mrs. Heflin.

A few weeks later we returned to that same restaurant and that same waitress made a point to let me know how lucky she thought I was and how she hoped to find a man just like him. The night that Buddy had proposed, this same waitress had been hovering around our table congratulating us and being very sweet, but I remember thinking that she should have backed away and not interrupted our time together. I know she was part of Buddy's plan to bring the roses, but she overdid it. On the way home I asked Buddy if he noticed and what he thought about her, but he brushed it off and said she just wanted attention. He was right about that.

CHAPTER 2
1961
The Big Day

THE SUMMER SUN WAS SHINING as I packed my suitcase for the two-day honeymoon. A few months after our "alone" date, it was our wedding day. Everything about the day is still very clear to me. The weather was a perfect 72 degrees, and the crepe myrtle and dog wood were in full bloom. We said our vows to each other on June 2, 1961, at Calvary Baptist Church in Starkville, Mississippi. Family and friends came to our small wedding ceremony and reception following. I wore a white satin dress and a veil. Like most girls, I had always known what kind of dress I wanted to wear.

Looking down the aisle of the church, I saw Buddy standing at the front with his father. The next thing I noticed was his dark suit, and then I saw him smile. I walked down the aisle to him feeling content and very happy. After we spoke to everyone at the reception, Buddy and I said "goodbye," and we were on our way to Biloxi, Mississippi. We got to the Ramada Inn and were given the keys to our room. I was so nervous about that night. I had a light blue spaghetti-strap nightgown which was so pretty. Buddy had never seen me without my make-up, so I was really nervous about that, too. I turned off the lights when I came out of the bathroom and he joked, "I was wondering when you were going to come out. I thought you had left." We laughed so hard. He had such a good sense of humor.

The next day we went to the beach to spend the day in the sun and the sand. In the evening we had an elegant dinner at a steak house. The tables were beautifully set with white table cloths, china, linen napkins, candles and a single red rose. We sat by the window over-looking the ocean, and I felt like life with this man was going to be exactly what I had always dreamed it would be. At nineteen years old, I knew Buddy wanted to start a career so that he could make money to take trips in nice cars and let me go shopping to buy pretty dresses. We talked about our future, but we both realized that we were just starting out, and neither of us had been used to having much more than what we needed growing up. So, our conversations were about planning for the future but not about how to get what we wanted right now.

After two days, we packed up to return home and start our lives together. On the way home, Buddy said that we would go on another trip later that summer or early fall. That never happened; however, the thrill of planning our future was no less exciting.

As for married life, I would miss him when he was at work and could not wait for him to walk in the door every night. Shortly after we got married, Buddy quit his job at Jitney Jungle meat department. His sister's husband helped him get a job at Manning Engineering Company as a land surveyor for future building sites, and he knew that if he went to college, he could do really well with this firm. The job was short-lived because Buddy was required to do a lot of traveling out of town, and Buddy preferred staying in his hometown.

When the manager at Jitney Jungle called six months later and offered him a raise, Buddy returned to the grocery store and his job as a butcher. We lived in a small two-bedroom house, and I loved decorating our home and buying the perfect new end table, lamp or picture as our budget would allow. I wanted to be the perfect wife. I had learned to cook really well, and I would prepare dinners every night just like I knew my mother did for my family. Of course, it was Miss Rosie who taught me and not my mother because I was only three when Mama passed away. I did not have the time with my mother that my older siblings had with her.

The lady who really taught me to cook, wash clothes and clean house was Miss Rosie. My father asked her to help out, and she came to the house every day at 6:00 in the morning to take care of us. Miss Rosie let me stand on the foot stool in the kitchen and watch how she made corn bread and fry catfish. She lived down the road, and I thought nothing of wandering down to her house on the weekends and knocking on the door. She always let me in. Rosie's passing and trying to grasp that I could never see her again felt as though I lost another mother.

The first meal that I fixed for my husband was mashed potatoes and gravy, fried chicken, fresh green beans and homemade rolls. For dessert, I made his favorite—banana pudding. Thinking back now it is so funny. Buddy started to gain weight a few months after we married, and even though he loved the meals, he was in the Army Reserves and had to stay in shape. My feelings were so hurt when he blamed the food and told me to stop cooking, but we were able to talk about it. I remember how sensitive I was, but I think that most young wives feel the same way. I continued to be a homemaker, ironing his sport coats and uniforms. The neighbors close to us were really helpful and fun. We would all get together on a Friday or Saturday night and have pot-luck dinners. Most of the neighbors were older than Buddy and I, had been married for several years, and they had small children. We were welcomed into the neighborhood with casseroles and desserts. I have such fond memories of the early days.

CHAPTER 3
1963
Our Family

I HAD BEEN THE DOTING WIFE, and ten months later, I was a doting mother. Our "Little John" was born in February of 1963. He was a snapshot of Buddy. I loved how proud Buddy was to be a father. Little John had his daddy's dark complexion, dark head of hair and the most innocent eyes I had ever seen. He melted my heart just like his father did that day at the pinball machine.

I loved being a wife, but nothing compared to the joy of being a mother. Having Buddy at home with me while we took care of our son and showed him to our family and friends made me very happy. This had been my dream, and I had a husband who was smart and funny and now this beautiful baby boy. I busied myself while Buddy was at work making sure the household was in top shape. I kept the checkbook and paid the rent and all of our bills.

Buddy always complimented me when I rearranged the furniture, and he noticed the clean house. We would eat dinner as a family and then play with Johnny. He was the cutest baby, and I was glad that Buddy adjusted to the new schedule so well. I made sure that the baby and I were on a good consistent schedule so that I could enjoy the baths, the naps, the feedings, and Buddy never failed to tell me that he appreciated me.

We did not know, of course, that we were having a son before he was born, but I remember that I wore a blue skirt and a white blouse to the baby shower. My cousin Shirley had the shower at her house where we played the usual games and opened the presents. When Little John arrived, I was more than happy to give all the baby girl presents to my sister-in-law.

I stayed home with Johnny for several months and then went back to work where I was a manager at The Holiday Inn. With beauty icons Elizabeth Taylor and Marilyn Monroe to look to for the latest fashions, I would dress up for my job, and Buddy would get so jealous of me. 1960s fashion called for false eyelashes, teased hair, stilettos and dresses with close-fitting waists.

As much as I admired Buddy's dark skin and green eyes, my black hair and blue eyes fascinated him. He thought that the men I worked for might steal me away from him because of their suits and good salaries. Their wives drove nice cars, wore expensive jewelry and shopped all day. Buddy worried because his wife had to work to help makes ends meet. Buddy was serious about his concerns which made him very uneasy at first, but deep down, I think he knew that he had nothing to worry about.

I focused on my family and our future. My dreams were achieved once I got married and started a family of my own. My mind wandered back to when I lost my own mother so early, and the sorrow I remembered inspired me to make every second count for my children. I never wanted Johnny to feel the sadness and loneliness of not knowing where his parents were or that feeling of being abandoned that had haunted me during my childhood without my mother.

Six months into my pregnancy with Johnny, Buddy began coming home later and later. I expected him at a certain time and could not wait until he opened the front door so we could spend the evening together having dinner and then watching TV or taking a walk. I never questioned him about what delayed him because I assumed he was working late to make more money for the new baby.

When the new baby first arrived, he was never a minute late, and our family routine lasted for about a year. We both loved Johnny and had so much fun together as a family that I tried really hard not to pressure him or ask too many questions when he started working late again and came home with no explanations. I knew what the nightlife scene offered in Starkville and the surrounding towns, and I could not imagine he actually preferred socializing with co-workers to coming home to our house and family. Southern women are taught two things: good manners and the Bible. I had been taught to be considerate and grateful, but I was beginning to feel more and more insecure. The feelings of being abandoned when I was a child because of my mother's passing resurfaced, and the hurt was unbearable.

When I finally questioned Buddy about where he went after work, he said that he was having drinks or playing poker with his friends. I continued to tell myself that everything would be okay, but I wanted my husband to come home from work to be with his family. If Buddy had known how upset I was on those nights when the dinner I made was ruined because he was out so late, I think he may have made an effort to come on home. Probably naïve, but I think it would have made a difference; I often consider what I could have done differently.

One thing I never questioned was whether or not Buddy loved the boys and me. He knew how to reassure me that we meant the world to him, so I was thrilled 18 months later when I learned I would be having a second child. Ricky was a beautiful little boy, and such a good baby. He and his older brother Johnny were always together laughing and looking out for each other. When Buddy was around, he was the best father and so protective. The boys loved to play outside, and their father made sure that they did not go beyond our fenced-in yard and into the street. The fishing gear in the garage was always ready, and the three of them would head out to the Oktibbeha County Lake and playground right down the road. They would return with crappy, catfish or perch, and I would cook them for our dinner.

We were married for a year and a half before having our first child. Buddy and I used to go out often to The Southern Air Club as a couple and spend time with other couples. We danced and listened to music. Other nights we dined with other couples at different restaurants.

My priorities changed to accommodate my newborn son and his needs after he was born. I loved every minute of taking care of Johnny and Ricky. I would give him baths and rock him to sleep. I was completely content with the duties of being a wife and mother; I had no desire to go out anymore because I would then wake up the next day without the rest I needed to devote the time and energy to my child.

Buddy started going out without me, and sometimes he was home in time to put Johnny and Ricky to bed, but his dependability became less frequent; I became more agitated. The discord in the house grew, and our conversations became contentious. As I lost my temper more and more easily, Buddy's disrespectful comments increased. We eventually crossed boundaries in our marriage but were too unsophisticated and young to realize the harm we were actually doing to our family. The distance between us was so deep that Buddy moved out, and we were not living together or even speaking for three months after Ricky was born. By that point we had only been married for three years.

CHAPTER 4
1964
The Secret Whispers Begin

BUDDY AND I HAD OUR SHARE of struggles, and we brought most of them on ourselves. Marriage means that your considerations about what you would like to do right now and in the long term have to take into account another person, who may have very different ideas about what that is. We discussed starting a family for almost two years before we decided to have children. Buddy and I were going to be devoted parents who were committed to family life and let the nightlife in Starkville, Mississippi, go on without us. The family-man lifestyle may have been too limiting for Buddy who loved socializing and meeting new people. Buddy also loved being a father to Johnny, but giving up the after-work cocktails with his friends entirely must have seemed too great a sacrifice. Being a mother fulfilled me completely, so I was thrilled but anxious when I learned we were going to have another baby. Buddy's reaction to the second baby renewed my faith in our marriage because I knew he was sincere about his promises to be the father he knew his children deserved.

Frustration and anger soon replaced the sense of hope I felt. Buddy resumed his irregular schedule and upset me time and time again by allowing what I assumed to be cards, bars, and friends to keep him away from our home. I began to scheme and devise plans so that I could catch him in action and force him to admit that he was wrong. I imagined a dramatic

scene that ended in Buddy's realizing that he needed
to change. I desperately wanted him to want to come
home to us.

As I increasingly spent more and more time
working and devoting my time to the children,
and Buddy spent more and more time working and
developing friendships at the bars, we naturally grew
apart. I resented his lack of priorities, and because I
could not depend on him, I automatically developed a
sense of independence that pushed him away. I started
to hear rumors about his wanderings about town and
indiscretions with other women. I had been told that
he had befriended a woman that he had met at The
Southern Air Club where he and I had spent so much
time together. I questioned Buddy about what I had
been told, but he insisted that nothing was going on
that I needed to worry about and that people were just
trying to make trouble and come between us. I wanted
to believe that he was telling me the truth and had not
been unfaithful to me, so I began to defend him and
deny the rumors. In hindsight, I should have known
better because of how young we both were. Regardless
of whether my intuitions were right or wrong, I have
no regrets about trusting Buddy; on the contrary,
believing in him despite the hearsay is something I am
proud of.

So, by the time I was eight months pregnant with
Ricky, I became distressed and concerned that Buddy
was living a life that I knew nothing about. Buddy
still had many of the same friends with whom he had
grown up, like Earl Burch and Gail Wofford; I met the
two of them not long after the time I first met Buddy

at the pinball machine. Those were names and faces I knew well and were frequent guests in our home. On one visit in particular, I learned that Buddy was keeping secrets from not only me but Earl Burch. Earl dropped by the house one evening around dinner time and was surprised that Buddy was not home. These two always knew where the other one was because they were always together. I panicked that night and resolved to find out for myself if the rumors were true. Earl Burch did his best to reassure me, so he stayed at the house until Buddy came home. Earl waited in the house watching TV while I took Johnny for a walk in the stroller. Finally, the lights from Buddy's car swept across the front windows, and I watched from the front door as Earl walked up to the car and opened the car door for Buddy.

Earl was most likely helping Buddy come up with an explanation. Earl knew that Buddy would not be telling me that the two of them had been together. All was explained by Buddy, and Earl's presence lightened the mood and distracted me. Even so, the dark shadows hiding secrets that undermined my belief in my husband were growing larger and braver, refusing to hide from my sight even in the day time.

The nightmare became all too real when Earl Burch, always a good friend of Buddy's, came over to my house and told me that if I wanted to confront Buddy, he would drive and accompany me to the bar. I no longer wanted to wonder where Buddy was and what he was doing. Earl Burch was going to drive me to the bar so that I could confront Buddy in action. That evening I dressed myself in my best dress, fixed my hair and makeup and was determined not to be made a fool of anymore. Earl could not drive fast enough to suit me because I dreaded seeing Buddy and debated about just going back home. Only three street lights delayed me from finding Buddy and seeing him face to face. I rehearsed again and again what I was going to say to him. I wanted him to leave the bar and come home with me so that we could talk and get this straightened out once and for all. When Earl and I got to The Southern Air Club, a bar on the Alabama state line, I spotted our new convertible.

Earl parked the car next to Buddy's, and even though I was eight months pregnant, I hopped out and found Buddy before Earl was able to open the door for me. I saw Buddy, my husband, sitting between two women, a blonde and a redhead. I stood behind the three of them and began to shout: "Is this where you have been all these nights? This is where you want to spend your time?" The speech I had rehearsed was thrown to the wind by my emotions of betrayal and anger. The music was so loud. I yelled things so awful that I cannot repeat them. One of the girls started to defend Buddy saying that they were just talking, and she reached out to rub my arm. Her face expressed a desire to console me. I reacted and screamed for her not to touch me, to get her hands off me. The other one laughed at me and muttered something in Buddy's ear about my being the "goody two shoes" he had told her about.

I have never understood why women do not defend each other in times like these. The two of them should have left so that Buddy and I could talk in private. But, neither of the women had any intention of missing the excitement, and I guess they enjoyed my husband paying for their drinks. I tried to tell Buddy that I did not deserve to be treated this way and that Johnny and the new baby deserved someone better. I told him that he could pick his things up from the front porch but not to ever come back home again. By this point, everyone at the bar was staring and listening.

Buddy glared at Earl and demanded to know why he had brought me there. Buddy told Earl that it was none of his business. Buddy had been drinking quite a bit, and he was so angry that he shoved me back and threw a glass of whiskey in my face. This confrontation was so humiliating for me, and I had to really look at him to see any resemblance of the man I married. Buddy glared at me, and I could see in his eyes how irritated and angry he was. Rage dominated his countenance, and it did not seem to faze him that I was standing there feeling so alone and embarrassed. My hair was dripping with the whiskey that he had thrown at me. He turned his back to me and ordered another one from the bartender. I stood there waiting for him to get up and reach for me, but Buddy never turned back around.

Earl put his hand on my back and said we should leave. When I got to the door that Earl had opened for me, I looked back and saw Buddy put his head down on the bar. He looked so dejected. He knew he was wrong but did not have the ability to think clearly enough to do anything more but drink. I was inconsolable and crushed. I got back into the car with Earl and started back home. When we got back to Starkville, Earl took me to Elise Johnson's house to get Johnny. She had agreed to watch him for me while Earl and I went to Columbus. Elise lived in my neighborhood, and her children were grown; she was so gracious with her time, her advice and her friendship. As soon as Earl's taillights disappeared in the distance, I stepped toward Elise's front porch and doubled over in pain. I managed to climb the steps to her front door, but the minute she saw me, Elise recognized what was happening and insisted that I go to the hospital. In all of the commotion, my water had broken, and I was in labor. Elise Johnson helped me into her car, and I drove myself to the hospital so that she could stay with Johnny.

I was scared and confused because the nurses were frantic and calling for doctors. I heard someone say that the baby was "breech." The labor lasted through that night and into the next morning. Thankfully Ricky was perfect except for the scratch on his nose from the forceps. He, too, had his father's dark complexion and hair. Ricky was the sweetest baby with the most precious smile. Looking into his face and seeing him look back at me was all that I needed to feel happy.

Earl got word to Buddy that I was in the hospital. I refused to see him and told Earl to tell Buddy that it was over. At this point in my mind, our marriage was just a piece of paper. Buddy did eventually come to the hospital to see his new son, and though I did not let Buddy know, I was relieved when he came to the hospital despite my telling him to stay away. Eventually, after three long months, Buddy moved back in our home and made all the right promises; I wanted to believe him, so I tried to deny the irreparable damage that had been done to our relationship.

Looking back, I consider the terrible scene we made at The Southern Air Club the beginning of the end for us. The bond of trust had been broken, and though I forgave Buddy for the humiliating experience seen by so many people in our hometown in the bar and asked him to forgive me for the things I said, our arguments became more frequent. The pattern of moving out and back in had begun. The forces of destruction were in motion. The night of the most lasting and traumatic damage that Buddy did to my trust happened when I was eight months pregnant with our second child. Ricky was born in September of 1964. Within three years after struggling with Buddy's broken promises, secrets and infidelity, I considered and finally made the decision to move far away and begin a life of my own. By the end of 1967 I was gone from Mississippi and living in Chicago. I returned once more with hopes of reconciling in April of 1968, and eight months after I left this time, Buddy vanished.

CHAPTER 5
1966
A Lesson in Forgiveness

IF BUDDY AND I HAD ONLY KNOWN then what I know now, protecting and treasuring the family that we created would have been priority. We were so blessed as a family. My boys were well-behaved, healthy, kind, and full of life. My husband was young and did not always live up to my expectations, but his two sons knew that he loved them. We had our family routine from the moment we woke up each day to have breakfast until it was time to go to bed, read a bedtime story and say our nightly prayers. Both Buddy and I were working and doing well at our jobs. I found a baby sitter to stay with Johnny and Ricky during the day by asking my doctor for a recommendation of someone I could trust. I was given the name of a young lady who had my pediatrician's complete trust, and even though I missed the boys on the days I worked, they really liked her and would hug her neck when it was time for her to leave in the evening. She cared for my children for several months; the boys seemed happy, and she began to earn my trust. I know that my boys looked forward to seeing her each day, but one day she snapped. I will never understand what caused her to brutally whip my little children, but the day is permanently etched in my heart and mind.

Buddy and I came home from work to find our two boys, Johnny (age 3) and Ricky (age 17 months), out on the front porch sitting in their little red rocking chairs. I got home first, and as I walked closer and closer to the boys, I realized that they were crying. The babysitter had wrapped each boy in several layers of clothes, towels and blankets, some of which were wet. She must have tried to do what she could to ease their pain before the severity of her discipline sank in and forced her to flee in fear. Buddy pulled into the driveway in time to hear, "Mama, she whipped us." The coat hanger that the babysitter used to punish my children was left in the garbage can. Bloody welts were on their backs and down the backs of their legs. They were both exhausted and terrified, and I felt the room begin to spin as what happened began to sink in. My heart was completely broken, and I felt like I was going to be sick. Buddy could not speak either.

At the time, we did not have a telephone in the house, and when I was finally able to ask Buddy what we were going to do, he hugged both boys who were afraid to move and in so much pain, and he left in the car without saying anything. I was terrified because I knew that Buddy had a gun in his car. I was shaken to the core by the thoughts that Buddy intended to kill her. But, when he could not find the sitter at her house, he went to the police. He filed a police report, and the police found the babysitter and arrested her; she was charged with felony child endangerment and served two years in prison.

The terrible story of what happened reached the news station; reporters were soon on my lawn with cameras. The newspaper published an article the next day about the incident. A picture of Johnny and Ricky showing the bloody welts on their backs was taken and appeared next to the article. I comforted my sons and did the best I could to ease their pain and fear. They were glad to see us because they had been left by themselves for some time. Although that day and the several days after, we were a traumatized family, the boys recovered quickly and seemed to forget the tragic day. Buddy and I did our best to cope, but the horrifying and shocking reality of what happened to the boys was still overwhelming. It was not very long until those little faces were smiling and laughing again; Johnny and Ricky healed a lot sooner than Buddy and I did.

I am thankful that the sitter was not at home that day when Buddy drove there to find her because I am afraid that he would have shot and killed her. Apparently, she fled to a friend's house, and the police officers found her hiding there. She tried to explain that she punished the boys for running too far away from the house and was afraid that they would get lost. I have no idea why she did this to my children. This lady may still be alive and living in Mississippi today.

Of course, I want to understand why the babysitter who agreed to care for my boys whipped them so severely. I have tried to think of any signs that I may have missed which would have given me reason to suspect she was angry or full of rage. I will always wonder what drove her to mercilessly punish my children.

I have forgiven her, but I still want to understand what prompted the action. Could she have harbored resentment from years of injustice against her family by racist white people? Resentment from wrong that finally caused her to lash out at Johnny and Ricky? Can I ever understand the source of her anger and frustration?

In doing research for this book, I have learned what a Mississippi Wind Chime is. I was thinking about the title—wind, whispers, etc., and I decided to hit one of the links. I will never forget what I saw--a black and white photo of white men and women and small children holding hands looking up at a tree. Hanging by the neck in the tree in front of them were five black men. The hearts and minds of those parents had to be steeled with prejudice for them to allow their children to witness this incomprehensible evil. Parents naturally want to protect their children not expose them by taking them by the hand and leading them to witness evil up close. By definition "prejudice" is an irrational hatred, so the hate felt by these people is never going to make any sense to others unless you share the same hate. The children exposed to the hangings in the photographs were taught to carry the inhumane hatred to the next generation without being able to reconcile or reason through their feelings. Now when I ask myself why the baby sitter whipped these children who loved her, I consider the injustice, prejudice and inequity experienced by the blacks in Mississippi in the 1960s. I may never know why she did it, but I have forgiven her.

When I was little, my father paid Miss Rosie to keep us during the day, and I needed to do the same for my boys while I was at work. Both black people and white people lived close to the house where we lived on Mr. Posey's Plantation when I was a child.

No one who worked for Mr. Posey had more money, or worked more or struggled less to provide food and clothing for their families, whether black or white. Sundays, however, taught me that we lived somewhat separate lives though. I knew as a child that Miss Rosie was black and although I was able to and did visit her home whenever I missed her, I knew that I was not allowed to go to her church on Sunday. At least, I was not allowed to go inside the church and sit down during the sermon. Whether someone told us with words or we just watched as the door closed in front of us, my older brother and sister, Leon and Lena, and I loved to sit on the front steps of their church listening to the hymns. The voices were beautiful, and we knew the words. When my mother was alive, church was not to be missed each Sunday, but after her death, my father was unable to take all of us to church because of the chores on the farm he had to do to keep us fed. We stayed home, and Daddy read the Bible on the front porch. Devastated after losing another mother, when Miss Rosie passed away, the three of us put on our best clothes and sat on the front steps of the church to say goodbye to our Miss Rosie. The preacher opened the church door and extended his hand to me: "These are the Hamilton children. Children, please come in." The preacher allowed us to enter on that one day because he knew how much we loved Miss Rosie. I am grateful that I was able to say goodbye to her by singing, "Miss Rosie is going home," over and over again with all of her family and friends.

The Old Testament speaks to future generations enduring the punishment for the sins of their ancestors: "The Lord is slow to anger, abounding in love and forgiving sin and rebellion. Yet he does not leave the guilty unpunished; he punishes the children for the sin of the fathers to the third and fourth generation" (Numbers 14: 18). The New Testament tells us that Christ, too, died hanging on a tree; He died for us on a wooden cross: "Christ redeemed us from the curse of the law by becoming a curse for us, for it is written: 'Cursed is everyone who is hung on a tree.' He redeemed us in order that the blessing given to Abraham might come to the Gentiles through Christ Jesus, so that by faith we might receive the promise of the Spirit" (Galatians 3: 13-14). Thankfully, I have been able to forgive the babysitter because of my faith nurtured in me from birth. I have often wondered about her. Had her brother died in a Mississippi Wind Chime that day? I am convinced something traumatic happened to her for her to brutally attack two innocent children. If this theory is close to the truth, then the babysitter probably looked to the same verses in the Bible to find comfort and peace and forgiveness; for Christians, remembering Christ's suffering on the Cross for our sins, endows us with the strength to endure our trials on Earth.

The extended family living in different states so far away were informed, and I heard my brothers' and sisters' voices crack over the phone as I did my best to explain to them what happened to Johnny and Ricky. The shock reverberated throughout our town, and neighbors tried to offer words of comfort. Children are so vulnerable, and though as parents we all do the utmost to protect them, life has unexpected trials for us sometimes. All I knew to do then is what I still do today-- have faith in a God who loves us and promises, "Jesus said, 'Let the little children come to me, and do not hinder them, for the kingdom of heaven belongs to such as these' " (Matthew 19: 14) and "I consider that our present sufferings are not worth comparing with the glory that will be revealed in us" (Romans 8:18) and "Bear with each other and forgive whatever grievances you may have against one another. Forgive as the Lord forgave you" (Colossians 3: 13).

Thanksgiving of 2013 has come and gone, and I am grateful and blessed for the early lessons from my father and Miss Rosie that taught me to raise my troubles to the Lord and ask Him for help. Turning to Him in the worst times is the gift of seeing past the present difficulties to the day when, "Now we see but a poor reflection as in a mirror; then we shall see face to face. Now I know in part; then I shall know fully, even as I am fully known" (1 Corinthians 13:12).

CHAPTER 6
1967
Smooth Talker

WE SPENT THE YEARS OF 1964-1967 separating and reuniting after the scene at the bar. I was so frustrated and unhappy, but the boys kept me busy and made up for Buddy's absence. He loved his boys and me, but the night he threw the drink in my face was so humiliating. Buddy may have started down a bad path way before I knew what was happening, but I definitely feel that the three months I refused to see him gave Buddy the opportunity to make connections with people he may have otherwise avoided.

I was so happy when we reconciled after being apart for so long, but the happiness was always short-lived; my happiness with family life was forced to confront the reality of secrets. For example, one specific time our lives seemed to be right back on track when Buddy informed me he had intentions of joining the Ku Klux Klan. I knew this group was nothing to joke about, but I just could not take him seriously listening to him act as though he would want to be a part of anything so evil. Where did Buddy meet men in the KKK? Why in the world would he need to join those people so full of hate? His parents and sisters would have never understood either. He must have been looking for a way to move ahead in the business world or maybe he enjoyed the political power of the group. At that time in the South, the KKK offered more to young men than just getting together and vocalizing their irrational hatred of different races. Buddy was not a racist man, nor had he been raised in that environment. When I realized that he was serious, I put my foot down about his having any connections with those men because their reputation was well-known, and I was not going to allow that white hood or cap or whatever it was in my home, and that was final.

I did, however, allow Buddy back into my life. The destructive pattern was in place; the back and forth, moving in and moving out was a constant until I moved to Chicago in 1967. Up until then, given his persistence and allure, I always let him move back in with us. The time apart was torment. I missed him terribly, and so did his sons. I wanted a family, and I could not bear the feeling I had when Johnny would ask where Daddy was. Buddy pleaded with me to forgive him, and that if I would, he would be the husband I wanted and the father our sons deserved. I knew that Buddy's father had been telling his son that he would regret losing his family, and that one day he would realize that keeping his family together would be the greatest joy in his life. Buddy's parents were loving and supportive but straightforward and strict when needed. When Buddy needed to be put in his place, his father knew just what to say. I had forgiven Buddy for the past, but it did not feel the same anymore. I only knew for certain that God never breaks promises and would continue to see me through.

Home had always meant everything to Buddy, and he felt very secure about letting me know how much he appreciated the home I was making for us. After dinner, on the nights he was there, he hugged me and did the dishes himself. Once the boys were born, he would hug me and add, "Thank you, Mama," so that the boys learned gratitude as he did. Ike and Sarah Heflin, Buddy's parents, respected each other. Ike set the example that fathers go to work, come home to their families and show how thankful they are for the blessings of what is most important in life.

On the nights when Buddy was there, we put the boys to bed, and the two of us talked. Perhaps because of having three older sisters, Buddy was sensitive and perceptive, easy to talk to. One night he told me how homesick and lonesome he was when he left for National Guard training, but he never acted like it around the other guys. I could not help laughing as Buddy pulled the blanket on our bed over his head and showed me how he covered up his face at bedtime in the barracks. Trying not to wake up the boys, I laughed out loud because every time he told the story, he added new details and exaggerated the way his eyes revolved around and his attempts to keep from crying so that the other guys would not know that he missed his mother.

How wonderful it is remembering listening and laughing and then falling asleep. In the morning we got up and made the bed together; Buddy on his side and me on mine.

At some point, the damage being done, the nights that Buddy did come home could not stop the woman he married from becoming increasingly more independent, so I pushed him away.

Somewhere along the way I know Buddy must have befriended the wrong people. The mention of KKK should have been a giant red flag. Rumors and suspicious coincidences thrive in small towns; I know this now, but I looked the other way back then. What I did acknowledge was that even though the innocence in his eyes never completely left, the carefree expressions and knowing winks began to fade.

Chapter 7
1961 – 1967
Not All Bad

EVEN THOUGH WE SEPARATED and reconciled too many times to count, Buddy and I managed to make some wonderful memories as a family during the next couple of years. Buddy loved being a father, buying them toy trucks and fishing poles. The three of them spent hours together once Buddy bought the boys their first Lionel train set.

I could barely keep up with where they were when Buddy was home from work. The three of them were always playing basketball or running around in the dark with flash lights. When one got a new pair of cowboy boots, all three got a new pair of cowboy boots.

Looking beyond Buddy's mistakes as a husband and seeing past to his gift of being a father was easy. I knew he had a father's heart. When he would come home, the boys knew the sound of his car in the driveway: "Mommy, Daddy is home! Daddy is home!" He could do no wrong in their eyes. I may not have known exactly what he was doing before he got home, but as soon as he walked through the front door, he was Daddy. We had many nights outside under the stars. Then the time would come for me to get the boys back inside the house to get ready for bed. Buddy would read to them and kiss them goodnight.

On nights when he would be later than usual with alcohol on his breath, I started to question him less and less. He and I would watch TV, and when I pressed him about anything specific with work, he would get unnerved and rigid. Eventually, I just did not want to know or care to ask. I resented being awakened at one o'clock in the morning because I needed to get up so early to get the boys ready for their day before heading to work myself. Looking back now, I can see how someone like him could get caught up in the dark side of business deals because he was personable, trusting and optimistic. He might have thought that he could keep the really bad part of illegal business dealings separate from the legitimate side of the business. He had such big dreams and so much personality. The allure of what could be would have been so appealing to a young man like Buddy. Buddy never offered me any explanation much less insinuate that he was involved in organized crime. These are theories I have after forty-five years of wondering but not knowing what happened to him.

Christmas time was always very special at our house. Buddy would buy me the most beautiful outfits. Stylish dresses, skirts and blouses hung in my closet. Growing up I had hand-me-downs, so the new clothes made me feel very special. I like to dress up every day, and he liked to tell me how pretty I was. He would leave small pieces of wrapped chocolate candy throughout the house for me to find during the Christmas holidays. I loved this side of him.

I remember one Christmas when we went out as a family and cut a live evergreen tree. The boys helped decorate it. I fixed homemade chili, and we sat down together to eat dinner and talked about the tree. This was going to be our tradition.

One summer Buddy took us on a trip to the Memphis Zoo. He alternated carrying the boys on his shoulders throughout the park. Sometimes we all went to the circus or a local fair. The boys would run around and come back panting trying to tell us what they saw or which ride was the most fun. These special days were magic, but Buddy had gotten involved in something that continued on in the background when he was not with us. This much I knew. But whatever was going on, was and still is, a mystery to me. I was very suspicious about the times he went away for a month with the National Guard. Buddy would change jobs often, and I was suspicious about why he moved around from job to job so often. He was always bringing home a paycheck, but he had connections with people who lived fast lives.

Back in those days, especially in the South, it was not unusual for women like me to not question their husbands. As long as we were being taken care of, we were happy. I knew I loved him and needed a man around the house. He was always a good provider, and I played the role I wanted to play. I was a good and submissive wife who tried not to nag but to look the other way. My identity was wrapped up in being a wife and mother to our children and that was what fulfilled me. We were a family, but we were not equal partners. After the dramatic confrontation at the bar that night, I knew sometimes it was better not to know than to shake up my life.

CHAPTER 8
1967
Too Much to Bear

I MANAGED TO STAY IN THE LIFE I was in until the boys got a little older. Buddy had gotten a job with his friend Earl Burch at the local Kroger. He was a good butcher and did very well. For a long time after Earl had taken me to the club where I found him drinking with the two women, Earl and Buddy did not speak. Buddy vowed that their friendship was over. Earl would call or come by, and Buddy refused to talk to him. As time went on, however, Buddy realized that Earl was trying to be a good friend. Buddy knew that Earl was a good friend and forgave him eventually. Buddy's friends were important to him, and I knew of the strong connections he felt because of the letters he wrote and received long after he came back home from his six-month National Guard training in South Carolina. His old friends were even more important to him.

Working with his childhood friend Earl Burch at Kroger went well for a while, but I have the feeling that behind the scenes, some illegal business transactions were going on in the upper management of the grocery store. Store meetings would go on very late, and Buddy would come home having been drinking. He started to drink more and more heavily. I was very uncomfortable with the direction he was heading, and I had to have a change. I now know that local businesses were run at the management level by organized crime. Kroger could have been one of them.

Even as a child I had always been brave and adventurous. The workers who worked on Mr. Posey's farm where we lived kept an eye on me for my father: "Don't worry about her Mr. Hamilton. She can usually be found hanging out with us." The big truck full of cotton choppers would arrive on the plantation, and I would wander off before my father realized I was gone from the front porch.

Now that I was married I wanted to be home and dependent on my husband, but the security was not there. My independent nature recalled my abilities to get along without anyone to guarantee that everything would be okay, and I had to consider my children. I really did not want anything to change the dreams I had of my own family, but Buddy was drinking more and more and was giving me less and less money to run the household. I started to evaluate my life so that I could be prepared if I were to be completely on my own. I got a job at the Downtowner Hotel as a cashier and hostess. It provided money that I needed to build a life away from Buddy. I felt compelled to leave the home I had known all of my life and move somewhere else. If I had not moved away when I did, I wonder if my boys and I would be missing just like Buddy is.

While working at the hotel, I met Joanne who proved to be a very good friend to me. Joanne knew someone who lived in Chicago who offered to help me find a job if I could just save enough money to get there and survive until I could get a regular paycheck. The idea of moving to Chicago seemed exciting and liberating. At first I kept the thoughts to myself because I never truly believed I would go. Once I began discussing my thoughts to my sisters and friends, the belief that I could really do it began to take shape. Buddy found out what I was considering and threatened to take the boys away from me.

We had been living in separate houses once again, but he would drop by to see the boys. Buddy must have seen the determination in my face because he stopped threatening me and tried to reason: "You can't take care of you and the boys by yourself." I was going to prove him wrong. He knew the day I was leaving and that there was no one who could change my mind. I had already discussed my plans with Ike and Sarah who offered to keep the boys whenever I needed them to.

For a short time, I did leave my boys with their grandparents. Day Care in Chicago was very expensive, and I was not really comfortable leaving them with anyone other than family even if I would have had the money to pay for Day Care. The community support systems available to children today were not available for working mothers in the 60s. I drove to Mississippi twice a month to visit them and talked to them on the phone every day. They missed me as much as I missed them, but I knew how well they were taken care of by Buddy's parents. Ike and Sarah and all of their aunts and uncles in Mississippi made sure the boys knew they were loved and would be well taken care of. As soon as the boys were old enough to attend public school, I enrolled them and made arrangements to drive to Mississippi and return with my sons. I was so proud when the day finally came for us to be together again.

Day in and day out I did not know when Buddy would find his way back home. I finally had enough money saved, so I packed up what little the boys and I needed and headed to Chicago. I had a map to follow and a future to find. I did not know anyone there, but I was determined to prove to myself that I did not have to depend on a man who was not determined to be a family man. Buddy probably thought that what he was doing was going to be short term, and maybe he drank to prove to his bosses that he was a team player. I needed him to prove himself to me. I was able to get a job with Western Electric as a lab technician quite quickly. It proved to be a very stable job that provided a lot more money for us than I could have ever managed to earn in Mississippi.

It took a little time to get used to Chicago. I was a girl from the hot, humid South now transplanted in a state with frigid temperatures and more snow that I had ever seen. The boys did not seem to mind, and I was just beginning to feel liberated. This new-found independence enabled me to find a confidence I had not had in a long time. Buddy found the self-confidence intimidating. He tried for six months straight to get me back home. I had moved out and back in so many times. Likewise, I left for Chicago and returned to Mississippi almost as much.

My brothers and sisters would try and help me during those times by letting my boys and me stay with them so that I could make plans. My sister Lena and her husband Bill drove to Mississippi one time and loaded the suitcases in the trunk. Buddy followed us in the car for a long time, but I kept telling Bill to keep driving. Finally, Buddy turned around. Bill would ask me if this is really what I wanted to do. I stayed with them for a while in Huntsville, Alabama, before I eventually went back home. Bill had met Buddy and really liked him. Of course, everyone really liked Buddy. They both lived in Starkville and would come into the restaurant where I worked. They went fishing together and were very good friends. We were all young couples trying to balance life and family. Bill and Lena had their two girls at the time, and I had my two boys. The seven of us drove on away from Mississippi, but I eventually went back.

Another time I left and this time I went to stay with my brother Ray in Michigan. Buddy started calling everyone trying to figure out where we were. Lena's husband Bill told Buddy where I was. Buddy knew that if he called Bill, he could find out because they were such good friends. Bill was sorry to upset me, but he said that if he were in Buddy's shoes, he sure hoped someone would tell him where his wife and children were. When Buddy called and I answered, I listened but reminded him that every time I came back to him, he would fall right back into his old habits. I would be home, but he would not be.

I think that Buddy was working for some people who demanded more than just eight hours a day. He would receive a paycheck from Kroger, but I believe now that he had been driving for people involved in illegal activities. I am not sure if it were drugs or guns or what. At the time I just knew that I could not depend on him to come home when he said he would come home. Several nights would be just like he promised;

he would come home, we would have dinner and then the boys would go to bed knowing their father was in the house.

Then one night and three subsequent days later, I did not know where Buddy was. He was never abusive, nor did he have a violent temper. I did suspect infidelity because there were so many nights when he did not come home. I would not see him for days, and when he would finally show up, he would not tell me where he had been. He did not want to be questioned; he wanted me to trust him and allow him what seemed to me to be a secret life. Otherwise, Buddy was a very good father to his sons.

All of the traveling around between the homes of my brothers and sisters with my two boys was both physically and emotionally exhausting. I remember times when I was so grateful for the kindness of strangers. At a train station one time, I was holding Ricky in my arms and Johnny by the hand. My arm had been so sore and had begun to cause me tremendous pain. Holding on to the boys though was first priority. A lady on the train looked at my arm and noticed a terrible sore. I had not noticed the actual spot, nor was I able to remember when the pain started. She quietly said that my arm was infected and that she was a nurse. That night after we got off the train, she took me to her office and lanced the place on my arm, cleaned and bandaged the sore. The scar from that procedure is still visible on my left arm; the scars left from the decision I made to leave Buddy are also still there, just not visible.

I began to think Buddy really did not want me anymore; I began to think that he just did not want me available to anyone else, so I grew very stubborn and independent. We were both so young, and I cannot help but think that if I had stayed with him, I could have helped him out of whatever trouble he was in. He would call again and again, but I had heard all of the promises before. He wanted the wife, the children, the cars, the home, the job and whatever else that he was keeping a secret from me. He would be convincing during our phone conversations, but I resisted.

One last time, however, after I had been in Chicago for a year, against everything my head was telling me, my heart said to return to Mississippi, and I did one last time. That was in April of 1968. I melted as I listened to his heart-felt pleas to come home to celebrate our birthdays together. He described the birthday cake, blowing out candles and making wishes, celebrating as a family, and how much it would mean to Johnny and Ricky. While I packed the car, I got distracted listening to the boys as they discussed getting to see their daddy; their excitement confirmed that I was making the right decision.

In writing this book, I have resolved to be as honest as I possibly can about the short time I knew Buddy Heflin. He vanished within months of my moving back to Chicago for the last time in April 1968. The days came and went without any word from Buddy — no phone calls or letters. I drove to Mississippi to find Buddy myself. His friends and family were as worried as I was. We all stayed in contact by writing letters and making phone calls. Days and weeks of waiting for word from Buddy have turned into forty-five years of waiting for news about Buddy. The idea that I would never hear from him again took a long time to sink in. I was hurt and defiant and determined and had been in this emotional state for years. Back and forth became the rhythm of my life.

On a sub-conscious level it had to be what I anticipated and expected. The end to this came abruptly. The next stitch in the pattern never came; time continued quietly and left the story of Buddy and me completely untold. The back and forth was finished but left incomplete December 31st of 1968. This cold winter day which closes one year and marks the beginning of a new one full of resolutions and optimistic promises for most people, was the last time that anyone ever saw Buddy Heflin.

CHAPTER 9
1968
The Note and the Last Straw

EARLIER IN THAT SAME YEAR before he disappeared on our final return home to Buddy, the boys and I had a strange and frightening experience. At the age of 23, I had just packed up the boys and headed back to Buddy.

As we were traveling on Highway 19, I noticed a semi-truck behind us. I slowed down so that he could pass by. He slowed down, too. I moved from the right lane to the left lane to see if he would just go passed us. He moved over as well and stayed right behind us. My heart began to race because I did not want to stop, and there were no places to exit. The trucker began getting closer and closer to the back of my car. I told the boys to keep their heads down in the back seat. I accelerated and held tightly to the steering wheel. As I would go faster, the truck driver would go faster. This went on for miles and miles. I was scared for all of us, but I was also furious. I saw an exit coming up so that I could get us off the Highway and onto the Interstate. Praying that I had enough gas to out run him, I took my chance and filed in with the other cars. The trucker could not maneuver as fast, so he went on. Who knows who else he terrorized on the road that night?

When we got back to Jackson, I was so glad to see Buddy. I had felt so alone on the terrible trip. I put my arms around his neck and hoped that I had shown him I had the courage to leave, and now he understood how the boys and I needed to be treated. Buddy had found us a comfortable home to live in. It was a three bedroom home with green shutters. There was a swing on the front porch and a big yard for Johnny and Ricky to play. Buddy seemed proud that he was making me happy.

We had been home about seven days, and as I cleaned the house and did the laundry, I planned the meals for the upcoming week. I surveyed the empty refrigerator, checked the pantry and made a list. As I settled into the driver's seat of Buddy's car to go grocery shopping, I noticed a white envelope sticking out of the visor. I reached up and opened it. I could tell right away that it was a woman's handwriting. This note had been written two days before I had gotten back home. This other woman discussed their recent lunch date a few days earlier, how much she loved him and how she could not wait to start a life with him: "Love always, Hannah Jo." The rush of emotion left me light-headed and breathless. Questions arose. Why had he dragged the boys and me back into this nightmare? Why couldn't he give up this other woman? Resolve and answers stabilized me. I was back in the same situation. I calmly confronted Buddy about the letter, but I knew what he was going to say before he did. I had heard the usual denial. By this point, I felt like I had been reading the same script over and over; I would read my lines, and Buddy would read his. I wanted to know who she was and everything about her, but I was too tired to really care. That day I built a wall around my heart and left Buddy for the last time. We would always share the boys, and he would always be a part of my life, but I was going to build a life in Chicago. After I packed, I left Buddy a note of my own on the kitchen counter that informed him very simply, "I'm not coming back." My heart ached for the boys, but I told them that we were leaving Daddy. The boys wanted to say goodbye, but I could not risk another chance to be lured back in.

I now remember that the letter had been sealed. I had opened the note and read it, but Buddy had not read it yet. I wonder if he even knew the letter was there. I can now see that he was being honest when he repeated, "What letter? Please tell me what you are talking about."

Part II:

survival

Instincts

Mississippi Whispers

CHAPTER 10
1968
Dangerous Secret Whispers

I HAD BEEN LIVING IN CHICAGO a few months and hearing that Buddy had acquired new friends in Jackson with shameless reputations. He still maintained his close friendships with people whom I knew well and trusted. Earl Burch worked alongside Buddy at Kroger in the meat department. His place of employment had not changed from when I left in April, but his place of residence had. Buddy called me one evening and told me that he was moving into The Baker Motel. Even though I was working and living in Chicago, the boys and I sustained regular, if not daily contact with Buddy.

The Baker Motel rented its one hundred rooms by the hour. This particular motel reminds me of motels I have seen in mob movies — owned and run by dangerous men. Why would he be living in a place like this? From what I had heard, the hotel was run by people who had well-documented criminal pasts and suspect criminal presents. I told Buddy that I would be afraid to go anywhere near that hotel and that he should try and find another place or live with his parents until he found something better.

I have always believed that he was probably allowed to live there rent free in exchange for driving his car in some illegal activity. Knowing Buddy, he naively trusted that the other men would look out for him and let him leave when he wanted to. Buddy was venturing into places far deeper than I could go to save him. I had to focus on our boys who were four and six years old. In a very short time after he told me about living at The Baker Motel, no one would ever here from Buddy Heflin again.

After living in Chicago for six months I returned to Mississippi to visit family. I called Buddy to give him the opportunity to see Johnny and Ricky before we headed back to Chicago. The boys were so excited to see him. The trees glowed with orange, red and yellow leaves. Front porches proudly displayed carved pumpkins and homemade witches and ghosts to welcome trick or treaters on Halloween.

Fall in the South is a time for families to enjoy the harvest of apples and pears so perfect for pies; and the vegetables from broccoli, beans, collard and turnip greens to okra, squash and cauliflower. In the air were the sights, smells and colors of baking and feasting, the warm wind had just a hint of cooler weather on the way, and then I heard the sound of Buddy's red convertible. Sitting in the passenger seat was Hannah Jo. We were still married. She glared at me as if she were the wife and I were the girlfriend. Hannah Jo was a pretty, thin girl with long straight brown hair and no makeup. I remember noting how different she appeared from me and my friends in the way we dressed, styled our hair and wore lipstick.

I thought to myself: "They deserve each other!" Buddy stepped over close to me whispering that he had no choice but to bring her with him. He shrugged his shoulders hopelessly as he explained how she had jumped in the car declaring that he was not going anywhere without her. The message she intended for me, I suppose, was that neither my children nor I were wanted back in Jackson. I pointed my finger at her and said sharply, "Remember, you are just the girlfriend. I am the wife!" Once Buddy said goodbye to the boys, he returned to the car where she waited. We watched them drive away having no idea that we would never see him again. That was April of 1968.

CHAPTER 11
1968
Ominous Signs at Christmas

THE CHRISTMAS OF 1968, Buddy went home to his mother's house and confided in his nephew Jimmy Bryant. Buddy's family knew what a big mistake it was to let his wife and two boys leave. They would tell me that he still loved me and was going to get us all back together soon. I believed them, and I believe that Buddy really did love us. Buddy told Jimmy that it was over with Hannah Jo.

Jimmy could tell that Buddy had not been sleeping or eating right and that he had been drinking. It could have been the stress caused by the fear of the people he had begun to associate and do business with. Jimmy only knew that Buddy wanted him to get in touch so that they could talk. Buddy was still calling me in Chicago and pleading for me to come back to Mississippi. He began attending church, and he had been baptized. Buddy knew how much that meant to me. I asked him about Hannah Jo, and he said that they were no longer together, but she was claiming to be pregnant. He insisted that there was a good chance that the baby was not his.

Immediately I thought of the boys and cringed but resolved that Hannah Jo's issues with Buddy were none of my concern. She had been in the car with Buddy the last time I spoke to him in person, and the look on her face that day definitely showed signs of desperation, not confidence or security. Chances are their relationship was under constant strain because of Buddy's real desire to keep his family together. Hannah Jo proved to me that she planned to fight for Buddy without regard for Johnny's and Ricky's feelings by accompanying him that day when the boys needed time with their father. She knew that her presence was distracting for Buddy which undermined the attention my boys wanted from their daddy. In my mind the risk returning to another even bigger mess was not worth it. No way would I ever come back to all of this!

So, from what I understand, after Buddy spent Christmas Day with his family, no one in the family heard from him in the days just before he disappeared. When he called to wish the boys and me a "Merry Christmas," I felt strongly that he was in trouble because he was not himself on the phone. His voice was tense, and he would pause for long periods of time without saying anything.

I learned years later in 2010 that as Buddy and Jimmy were leaving to go home after Christmas dinner, Buddy pleaded with Jimmy to come see him at The Baker Motel. Jimmy did go visit his uncle, but it was after Buddy came up missing. I did not hear Jimmy's account of his visit to The Baker Motel until 2010. The fact is that Jimmy showed up at the front desk, but the clerk told him that no one had seen the man in that room in several days. She gave him the key so that he could go check for himself. That is when Jimmy found that the room had been trashed.

Jimmy told me this because he wanted to let me know before he died. Jimmy had been very sick for a long time, and he passed away in 2012. I knew his time was short when he accompanied me to Captain Raymond Delk's office in 2010. Captain Delk was head of the MFBI, and I made an appointment to discuss the new information I had learned from Gail Wofford, Buddy's close friend from childhood, and Jimmy Bryant's account of his visit to fulfill his promise to visit his uncle at The Baker Motel.

We found out that the last time anyone had talked with Buddy was New Year's Eve which was the beginning of 1969. Buddy might go a few days without calling, sometimes weeks, but we had always touched base about the boys. Three months had gone by now, and he seemed to have disappeared from the face of the earth. I contacted everyone I could think of with no success. Bill Harpole was the Deputy Sheriff in Starkville, so I called him and asked him what he knew. He promised to investigate and let me know. I called him and other investigators in both Starkville and Jackson again and again, but I would always get the same response, "Not a word." I try not to, but I cannot help but think the case was dismissed or the evidence was covered up the first day his absence was reported to authorities. Buddy's sister Annie Belle made several calls and wrote letters herself trying to find out about her brother, and she received two letters from Dewey Weems, Supervisor of Identification Bureau; one letter is dated February 8, 1971, and the other one is dated January 7, 1972.

In the second letter, Buddy's sister asks for someone to give her any news at all: "Reference your letter dated December 31, 1971, this is to advise we have been unable to ascertain any further information concerning Mr. Heflin." That would have been the day after spending the third Christmas not knowing what had happened to her brother.

Alexis Heflin

CHAPTER 12
Early 1969
Missing Person's Report
"in absentia"

A PERSON MAY BE MISSING DUE TO his own decision to leave home, live somewhere else, and with a new identity start a new life. Death, whether the consequence of natural causes, random mishap, mass disaster or murder, therefore, is not automatically assumed by authorities. A fatal accident can happen when a person is far from home and without identification leaving authorities with a body that no one claims. The deceased's family and friends publicize the missing person's description on bulletin boards, milk cartons, websites, and in many cases, the end result, though heartbreaking, provides closure to loved ones. But without direct proof of a missing person's death, such as finding remains, a person may be declared "legally" dead as in Buddy Heflin's case because a person has been missing for an extended period of time without any evidence that he is still alive, or when the circumstances surrounding a person's disappearance overwhelmingly support the belief that the person has died.

Buddy's parents filed a missing person's report on their son within two weeks of his failing to come home or contact them. The ominous cloud surrounding Buddy because of his unusual behavior at Christmas foretold that he had gotten himself in big trouble. The last time I was with Buddy in April of 1968 I could tell that he had secret concerns that he would not discuss. The innocence in his eyes never completely left, but the carefree expressions and knowing winks began to fade. Before I left for Chicago in 1967, the after-work meetings at Kroger lasted longer and into the night; relaxing on the front porch or learning the words to the latest Elvis song was replaced with blank stares and made-up excuses for where he had been. I left with the boys many times and returned to him because he promised to change back. He was so happy to see me and the boys every time.

The last time was no different, but the light in his eyes now reflected fear. He very quickly grew quiet and seemed almost bewildered and disoriented. Now I wonder if he knew that he could not keep his promise to change back. I think he did. Buddy knew that the days of singing Elvis and laughing before falling asleep were over. He was in too deep. Why else would his good friend Earl Burch commit suicide months later in 1971? I believe that either Earl participated in or witnessed his best friend's death. That explains why he called Buddy's mother on Christmas Day in 1970.

I have recently talked with one of Buddy's sisters; I called to find out more about him when he was a child. I was hesitant to call because I can only imagine what emotions are disturbed recalling memories of her little brother. Very likely Buddy's disappearance was preceded by a violent death. Very likely Buddy was terrified of the people who actually killed him and knew them and what they were capable of very well. The months before he vanished must have been hellish for Buddy. Ike Heflin, Buddy's father, passed away from a heart attack within months after his son stopped calling and coming home.

Sarah Heflin and her three daughters were then left to live with the mystery and the loss of both their father and only brother. All of Buddy's sisters had gotten married relatively young and were no longer living in their parents' home, but the family was close, and the girls' attention was naturally focused on their own families but diverted and divided out of concern for their mother. Sarah Heflin remarried; chances are that necessity left her no choice. This marriage was short-lived because Sarah shot and killed her second husband shortly after they got married. The reason she killed him is because he was abusive. Neighbors tell stories that corroborate her testimony. Sarah Heflin was convicted and sent to Parchman Penitentiary for murder. My heart breaks when I think how this woman's life was ripping apart at the seams, and the investigation into her son's disappearance was dismissed. Sarah Heflin went to her grave knowing that no one in the family feels anything but genuine love, acceptance and understanding for this woman who cherished her home and the family that belonged to her at one time. She paid the penalty for her crime, but there has never been justice for her son.

Parchman Penitentiary also known as Parchman Farm is still in operation in Starkville, Mississippi, where everyone with whom this story has a connection grew up. At around age seven I visited Parchman Prison with some of my siblings and my father. More than anything my father desired and meant for us to stay out of trouble. The prisoners were chained together at the ankles, and sun-up to sun-down, they worked the fields of the farm. Working so close with hoes, shovels or scythes, the individual gray and white striped uniforms blurred into one powerful object which performed one powerful task. My father's third cousin served a life sentence for a murder he committed as a young man. The visit was intended to make clear what happens to people who get into trouble. Surprisingly, none of us ever did get into any trouble. The then old man sat waiting for his visitors and smiled when he saw my father approaching. His inoperable hands were clenched in permanent fists from arthritis; his elbows seemed pinned to his sides. As we walked away, I noticed the dirt floors and his bare feet. His eyes were so kind and bright underneath the silver hair.

While doing research for this book that will hopefully get people to come forward with information about Buddy Heflin's disappearance, my niece Valerie Leary struggled to find out anything about this prison that is mentioned in the Social Security documents. The names of many people associated with Buddy in those last days have criminal records with time spent at Parchman: Red Davis, and Doris and Keith Warren. Recently my sister Lena was recalling her memories of Buddy because he and her husband spent time together fishing and talking back in the days when all of us were newly married.

Bill had encouraged Buddy to continue taking classes at Mississippi State University where he was attending college. Lena remembers visiting the prison as well. Valerie, her daughter, was listening intently and corrected her mother's pronunciation, "Pardimon Prison?", she questioned. Lena eyed her curiously and acknowledged, "No, Parchman." The name of the prison is misspelled in the Social Security document. So, that mystery is solved at least. The history of Parchman Prison is notorious, and housed The Freedom Riders in the 70s who rode the bus to protest Mississippi's continued refusal to follow the desegregation of transportation between states mandated by the Federal Government. Poor Mississippi, known for ignoring what is right and holding on the tightest to what is inhumane, has lagged behind the other states in almost every category.

CHAPTER 13
1970
Earl Burch Wants to Talk
on Christmas Day

I HAD BEEN LIVING IN CHICAGO two years when Buddy's mother called me again. She had new information. The last call was to tell me that Buddy's car full of bullets holes, shattered glass and blood stains had been found at a truck stop. This time she tells me that Earl Burch had called Buddy's sister Frances on Christmas Day; it was 1970. He wanted to let her know that she and everyone else should forget about Buddy because his body had been thrown in the Mississippi River somewhere around Vicksburg. We called the authorities immediately, but when the investigators spoke with Earl in person, he would not confirm any of what he had said to Frances. I was so suspicious of the police officials that I was convinced that they had threatened him if he continued to say anything else. Why would he completely change his story? He would not have called on Christmas Day and said this. Earl Burch and Buddy were close friends. No matter what I thought or said, the investigation once again stopped cold.

Four months later in April of 1971, Buddy's mother called again to give me the tragic news that Earl Burch had taken his own life. He had shot himself at home. The police and others had been questioning him about Buddy's disappearance since only a few months had passed. The blood-stained car belonging to Buddy had been found less than a year before. Why would Earl Burch commit suicide? Had he been guilty of something? Was he afraid of something or someone? Had he feared capture or imprisonment more than death? Had someone threatened his family? What if his death was not suicide, just made to look like suicide?

I pleaded with Deputy Harpole to question Earl's wife. He told me that his department had done all that could be done. He insists that he had questioned Earl Burch several times, and that he had also talked with Earl's wife. I felt so strongly that someone had to know something more. This was the closest I had ever been to any answers, so I picked up the phone and called Earl's wife myself. The first time I called she answered. She did not want to talk to me or answer my questions. It seemed to me that she was scared. She was a grieving wife, and I tried my best to be considerate.

At the same time though, I was angry with her because at least she knew for sure what happened to her husband. She knew that he was dead and could receive benefits to help her children and herself. She possibly knew more about Buddy that could bring closure for us, but she offered nothing. Why wouldn't she talk to me? What had happened in Mississippi to cause my husband and Hannah Jo to disappear, and Earl Burch to kill himself. Not long after that another friend of Buddy's disappeared, Red Davis. Buddy was missing and the evidence continued to mount that he had been murdered and the police officials were playing a part in the cover-up. Hannah Jo was missing, Earl Burch kills himself, and now Red Davis? No one was talking.

Not to me at least. Surely something would surface because of all the Mississippi missing person's reports that were piling up!

The fact is though that no missing person's reports had been filed except the one that Ike and Sarah Heflin filed on Buddy. Was I supposed to believe that these events were all isolated and unrelated?

In Chapter 22 of this memoir, I detail Gail's account of a secret she had been keeping for forty years because she had been afraid to tell anyone. Facing death from heart disease in 2010, Gail decided to reveal what she knew about her dearest childhood friend's last days.

Was it not now obvious that everyone Gail Wofford named had been connected in some underworld criminal activity and as a result, each had three options left. Either you could be murdered, you could disappear and hide from the people at the top, or you could take your own life.

Alexis Heflin

Chapter 14
Chicago 1971
Desperate Times, Desperate Measures

EVENTUALLY I ENDED UP AT ODETTE'S, the local fortune teller, where I was living in Chicago. Although I never knew anyone in Mississippi to go to a fortune teller, a lot of people I knew in Chicago talked about going frequently. My father would have said that going was not a good thing to do. I felt fairly certain that I should avoid anything other than what is taught in the Bible. Bible prophecy foretells the end times, and I needed information about where Buddy was and what happened to him. If the Bible does not discuss a particular topic, I believe that it is information I do not need access to. I genuinely did not even believe in the psychic ability of fortune tellers myself, but I began listening to the stories that my friends would tell about Odette. Co-workers, neighbors and friends declared that Odette was eerily accurate, and they urged me to see what she knew. I knew better than to ask anyone in my family for advice; any hint to them about what I was considering would have been returned with, "Absolutely not." More and more though, I began to want to go to see if she could tell me anything about Buddy.

In the 1960s' South, we accepted the stereotyped image of gypsies and fortune tellers as truth; they wore low-cut blouses while dancing around seductively to the music of guitars and tambourines, telling stories about the future by reading palms in a drug-induced delirium. We imagined the roaming bands of people living in secluded clans in the middle of nowhere while they learned the art of witchcraft and devilry. The men among them were expert con artists. The stories we heard were rife with tales such as these that encouraged all the stereotypical images. However, in Chicago in the 1960s and still today, fortune tellers shop, attend church, work in restaurants and play musical instruments in concert halls throughout the Chicago area; in other words, they are real people, not stereotypes, who originated from Romania, and as did large groups of Hungarians and Serbians, immigrated to the Southeast Side steel mills of Chicago in the late 1800s.

I walked into the old house and entered the front room. The floors squeaked with every step. She had candles lit everywhere, and the overhead lights were very dim. I saw a chair covered in a black cloth and heard her voice ask me to take a seat. The woman across the table was able to see me from the moment I walked in, but I was only able to see her after my eyes adjusted to the darkness. Something made me stay even though I was thinking about getting up and running away. She asked me a few questions and commented that I was a very attractive lady who had three children. I placed my hand on the Bible as she directed, but this seemed very out-of-place.

I corrected her. "I have two children."

"No," she said, "you have two, but you lost one. So, that makes three."

I could not believe this. It was true that I'd had a miscarriage when Johnny was three months old, but I had never told anyone. She went on to say that I had problems with the last pregnancy. I was amazed that she knew these things. Odette asked me if my husband was sick or in trouble. I told her that I did not know. I will never forget the look in her eyes through the candlelight as she turned over a card and said, "Tragedy is coming."

I was twenty-five-years old when I went to see Odette, so the experience was very disturbing to me. I went home that night and tucked the boys into bed. We said our prayers. When we finished, Ricky looked up at me and said, "Don't forget to pray for Daddy!" We prayed for Daddy every night thereafter.

CHAPTER 15
1971
Chance Encounter

DURING THE YEARS AFTER Buddy's disappearance, I always did my best to stay in contact with his family. The boys and I would make the trips to Starkville twice a year to see everyone. I remember Buddy's father trying to make things better for me when I would move out. Ike would come over to see the boys and offer to stay with them so that I could go out and get groceries. He was disappointed in the way Buddy was acting, but like all of us, his dad felt that in time Buddy would grow up and take responsibility as the man of the house. We all knew that Buddy loved his two sons more than anything else. When Buddy and I were first married, Ike wanted to know every time that I made fried chicken, mashed potatoes, and green beans. He said that mine was the best fried chicken in the state.

Both of Buddy's parents were always supportive of me, and I appreciate knowing that they liked me. Too many times in-laws can create tension in a young marriage by expressing disapproval and finding every excuse to criticize what the new wife is doing. That could not be further from what Ike and Sarah were doing. Ike did not live much longer after his only son disappeared under such mysterious circumstances, and he would have known more about the possible violent end Buddy faced than he would tell either Sarah or me.

Because they were so good to me, I wanted Johnny and Ricky to bond with Buddy's family. In 1971, over two years after Buddy's disappearance, on one of the trips to see them, something unbelievable happened. We were traveling along in the Volkswagen on Highway 55 South in Missouri telling stories and singing songs when the Volkswagen stalled. I acted quickly and got the car to the side of the road. The boys hopped out, and I started to panic. It was so hot, and there was no telling when the next car would pass by! I spotted a building and parking lot off in the distance, so instead of waiting for the next car, I made the decision to leave the car and our luggage and trek across the open field with the two boys and ask someone in the building for help. We came to a fence that we would all have to climb when Johnny said, "Mom, look at that plane!" A twin-engine plane was circling above us. Just then it started a frightening descent toward us! What was happening? It looked like it was going to crash. The plane landed on the highway just down the road from us, and the pilot got out and started to walk in our direction. My heart was in my throat. I was stranded on the highway trying to go find help only to be completely caught off guard by the plane that flew out of the sky out of nowhere. As it turned out, the building off in the distance was a small community airport. The pilot spoke to the boys first as they were staring with awed expressions.

"Hi, guys. Got car trouble?"

Before I could speak, Johnny said, "It won't start anymore." The pilot stepped over and lifted the hood.

"You three definitely have a problem," he said, "how far do you have to go?"

I explained that we were headed to Starkville, Mississippi, which was still several hours away.

"Let's see what we can do," he said calmly. "You and the boys will burn up out here. Let's get you over to the airport to see what's going on." Before he called a mechanic to come and tow our car, he radioed a man at the airport to come and pick us up. The men from the airport had the car brought to the plane hangar. The mechanic knew exactly what the car needed, but no one who had the part was open that Saturday. It would be Monday before they could get in touch with anyone else.

I was stranded in a strange place with strangers, and even though they could not have been more polite, I was not able to relax. The boys were fine, and they enjoyed being shown around the airport and sitting in the different planes. As hard as I tried to stop worrying, I stayed right by Johnny and Ricky and pretended to be having fun, too. I did not tell anyone that I did not have enough money to stay in a motel for two nights. I would have nothing left. I was now going to have to pay to have the car fixed, but I was too afraid of the answer to even ask how much it would cost. As all of this was going through my head, the pilot came over and said that he would take us to a hotel down the way. We drove up to a hotel called The Land's End with accommodations for $49 a night. We could afford that depending on the price for the car part to be replaced and installed. When we arrived at the hotel, the pilot introduced us to the staff at the check-in counter. This man could not have been nicer to us.

As soon as we settled into our room, I phoned my sister and told her what happened. She was very concerned about us and offered to come and get us or wire money through Western Union. She asked me if I was scared because she probably could hear it in my voice. I told her that I thought we would be fine and that we would see her on Monday. After saying the words, I did begin to feel much better.

Monday morning came, and the mechanic had found the part at an auto supply 100 miles away. I had to check out before 11 am or get charged for another day. Our money was getting really tight. The pilot showed up at the hotel and asked the boys if they would like to fly to get the part? What could I say? The boys were so happy! I agreed, and we all piled into the plane with six seats. We buckled the boys in, and I found myself in the co-pilot's seat. Little did he know that I had never been in an airplane. I had climbed into a plane with my two boys and flown away with a complete stranger. Perhaps an angel had sent him because either this man was heaven sent or my two boys and I were in great danger. I prayed harder than I ever have during that flight. During the flight he kept the boys' minds occupied on the scenery in the area. They had their faces against the windows smiling big smiles. I took a deep breath and then realized how alive I felt. I felt really alive.

When we returned with the part, they had the car fixed within an hour. It was now time for us to go.

The pilot reached over and mentioned that he wanted to pay for our stay at the hotel. I could not accept his offer. He had done so much already. I paid the bill and told Johnny and Ricky to wait for me while I took one last restroom break before starting out. I thanked everyone and got into the car. At the next gasoline station, I found $200 folded with a note which read, "I was glad to help you and your boys, and if you need anything, just let me know." We were never to see him again, but I now knew our lives would be different. I was beginning to feel like myself again after so many years. Whether it was the intense fear or the thrill of flying in a plane or the unexpected experience of staying two nights in a hotel, I do not know. I started taking Johnny and Ricky to a local café called Tops Big Boy every week and watched as they devoured strawberry pancakes, bacon and hot chocolate. We would all get excited planning for the next time and remind each other about our new plans. We began going to the theater to see Walt Disney movies that were advertised on TV. I decided that I would go out to dinner sometimes.

The boys were handling what life had thrown at them so well. They had grown into young gentlemen. I had been blessed that they had inherited my good traits and Buddy's good looks. I could see their father come out in them at different times, and it always made me laugh. When they were teenagers, I told them that I would give them a $5 allowance for keeping their rooms straight. They were excited about this because they wanted spending money for the movies. I noticed what a great job the boys were doing with this responsibility. Actually, I was amazed at how clean their rooms were. So, my motherly instincts were right. I later found out that the smooth talkers had invited their girlfriends over from school to help them clean. If I had found out at the time, the boys would have been in serious trouble, but since it was after the fact, I could not help but smile and see their dad in them both.

CHAPTER 16
Early 1970s
Life Goes On

IN 1967 AT THE AGE OF twenty three, I was the mother of two, and I put my trust in a friend who had a friend in Chicago saying that she could get both of us a job. Instead of working here and there as I was doing in Mississippi, the job in Chicago provided benefits and retirement.

I had already been in Chicago two years when Buddy disappeared in Mississippi. I had tried to do what I could to find out what happened to Buddy. A missing person's report had been filed on Buddy with Deputy Bill Harpole. Police officers knew that his truck had been identified, and eye witnesses reported seeing bullet holes and blood in the truck but no sign of Buddy. Deputy Harpole had gone to school with Buddy and promised to do all he could to investigate Buddy's disappearance. Every week after that, I would call the Starkville Sheriff's Department to see if there had been any news. Bill Harpole would say the same thing every time: "No change. I haven't heard a word." I heard these words over and over again.

Just because Buddy was missing did not mean that life had come to a stop for me. The bills had to be paid. Because he was missing, I had no child support, no insurance money and no social security check to rely on. I was the sole provider now, so I wanted to find a steady job that provided what we needed as a family. The Social Security check began to come only seven years later when Judge Windels declared him legally dead. By that time, the boys were almost out of high school.

In 1967 Buddy was still living in Mississippi but I had moved to Chicago and found a place for my boys and me to live. I was driving around the different neighborhoods and saw a dark brick duplex for rent. The landlady's name was Mrs. Faxon, and she welcomed the boys and me with open arms. She was a God-send. The boys, after a time, adopted her as their grandmother. Johnny and Ricky were five and three years old, and Mrs. Faxon allowed them do chores for her. In return she would bring hot chocolate over to the boys. I welcomed her friendship.

Johnny had to settle into a new school when we got to Chicago. It was so much larger than his previous school in Starkville, and he had little time to adjust. I had no choice but to put Ricky in daycare for a short time. There was no time to worry about anything but finding a job. In those days, very few mothers left their children in daycare, but I had to. I traded our Chevy convertible for a more affordable Volkswagen. The convertible was more expensive to repair and unsuitable for the winter months. Chicago winters require a car capable of traveling in deep snow. The first month's rent was due on the day I received my first paycheck from Western Electric.

The first few weeks were eye-opening. I began my first day in assembly and worked so hard that I made

100% production. I had always worked really hard since I was a child, the youngest of seven children. I picked cotton one week to earn money to go to a movie when I was seven, and by the end of the week I had picked an entire bale. Daddy did not mean for me to work quite this hard, but he was very proud of me when I did. The pace I was working now did not sit well with my new co-workers who had been there longer and settled into a routine. That first week my supervisor pulled me aside commending me on my performance, but in not so many words told me that it was not necessary to work so hard. He told me that I could slow down the pace. He was such a friendly man and wanted me to feel at ease and not worry about losing my job, but I did not mind working at a fast pace. I told him that I appreciated his kind words. The site manager recognized the job I was doing, too, and he gave me $1.00 an hour raise. I was thrilled! I needed the job because I needed the money for my boys. I was hoping and praying that Buddy would come back from wherever he was and help me. I wavered between knowing I needed to separate myself from Buddy and his troubled life and wanting him to rescue us.

Several weeks had passed since anyone had seen Buddy when I got a phone call from Buddy's mother. Her voice on the other end made my heart jump. Buddy's parents Sarah and Ike had been contacted and told that the car Buddy had been driving the last time he was seen, had been found at a truck stop. She told me that it was Barkey's Truck Stop in Bonvina, Mississippi. The car was ripped with bullet holes, and there were blood stains. I gasped for breath. There were no more answers to my questions. She told me all she knew, and so I remember putting the phone back down on the receiver overwhelmed by feelings of helplessness. Jimmy Bryant, Buddy's nephew, spotted Buddy's truck at the truck stop. "Inexcusable" and "indefensible" are words that come to mind when I consider the police officers whose job it was to actively look for Buddy. All of us who knew and loved Buddy, especially his parents, agonized about his physical condition, emotional state, and every day we struggled not knowing whether he were dead or alive. Buddy's abandoned truck stayed parked on the pavement testifying with shattered glass and punctured metal that gunshots had been fired. Anyone curious enough to walk closer could see blood stains. Jimmy drove a truck for a living spending countless hours on the road. He passed by the truck for months until one day it was gone. Buddy's truck was the first evidence that pointed to foul play. Buddy had worked in the meat department at Kroger on New Year's Eve 1968. After that, he disappeared. Ike suffered a heart attack and died shortly after his son's disappearance. His three sisters, Frances, Anna Belle and Willie Mae are still alive, living in Mississippi.

After a minute, I picked the phone back up and called Bill Harpole, the deputy sheriff in Starkville. I wanted to know what this new information would mean to the investigation. I was really surprised when he did not seem more disturbed and concerned. I expected his voice to be loud and anxious. In a very nonchalant tone, he said, "We are looking into all the current leads." I asked if anyone knew where Hannah Jo Allred was. I found out that she is now missing, too. I put the phone down and began to cry. What would I tell the boys? All I had was a missing person's report.

I continued to call weekly for months getting the same answer. I was beginning to wonder if they just did not care or if they had reasons for wanting the case to disappear, too. I have been suspicious of the authorities involved since that time. Soon, I contacted the sheriff's office in Starkville less often; eventually, I thought, "One morning I will wake up and realize that Buddy is not going to be found alive, nor is the mystery surrounding his disappearance going to be solved." Accepting the obvious confronted me out of disappointment and frustration. Then, the reassuring reality that sometimes individuals who have been missing for years returned to their families, washed over my mind like the first rain in spring. How could I abandon all hope? For years every time the phone rang, the thought that this was the call with answers about Buddy raced through my mind.

CHAPTER 17
1972
Scared

THE BOYS WERE GROWING UP in Chicago and making friends. They were good boys, and I made sure that they had a firm foundation in the Bible. That was one of the fondest memories I had of my mother, and I wanted my boys to have fond memories of me in this way, too. Johnny had even won a beautiful new Bible for learning verses in his Sunday school class.

My sister Margie tried to help me as much as she could. She would come get the boys in the summer and let them stay with her so that I could have a little break. The boys loved their trips with their aunt and uncle because they had two boys as well, and they lived in Flat Rock, Michigan. I would try to get up there at least once a month so that the boys could see their cousins. Margie and her husband knew that I was having a hard time financially, so she always made sure that Johnny and Ricky could have a summer vacation with her family. I stayed close with my family and Buddy's family so the boys have strong family ties which provide a firm support system. It never failed to hit hard, however, when they would ask where their Daddy was. Johnny had been old enough to remember his dad.

Important as it was for the boys to have close ties with the family, I also wanted them to form good, lasting friendships. I was very fortunate that the neighborhood boys were good influences on my boys and gave them someone to talk to. Johnny had made a friend with a boy named Billy. They would spend the nights together and go on adventures. Billy would ask Johnny why his dad never came to school plays or sports games. It would really bother Johnny on those days that were special for fathers and sons. I did not know what to say except that he had gone away, and no one knew when he might come home. Ricky made a friend who lived down the street named Paul. Depending on the time of year and the playground provided by nature, the boys were ever ready for the next adventure out of doors. Riding bikes throughout the neighborhood provided the transportation for each excursion.

One evening all four boys had gone out together on their bicycles. It was getting late, and motherly instincts were telling me that something was not right. No one had heard from the boys, so I drove my car through the streets calling out their names. All that was racing through my mind were the worst possible scenarios. I got out of the car and started down the trail. There was not a trace of any of them. I began to sob. I was powerless against and paralyzed by fear. It was dark outside, and I could not find my boys. Not again. Where were they? Just then I heard familiar voices in the distance. I looked up to see Johnny and Ricky along with their two friends. My heart melted, and now there were tears of joy.

When we got back home, I told the boys how worried I had been. I did not sleep that night. The experience had dragged up feelings of separation and abandonment again that challenged my capacity to cope. I really wanted some closure, to feel complete. I had gotten my life squared away in Chicago, but distress from my half-finished old life presented itself again and again.

CHAPTER 18
Chicago 1977
The Boys and I Wait

EIGHT YEARS HAD PASSED BY with no news of Buddy. I was working a steady job in Chicago at Borg Seal Master Bearings as an assembly-line technician and was able to support the three of us. My landlady Mrs. Faxon had passed away, so once again my boys and I packed up our belongings and moved to a new place closer to my work.

The year was 1977, eight years since Buddy had been seen, so I contacted an attorney in Chicago, Peter Grometer. He would be able to help me start the proceedings to have Buddy declared legally dead. Based on the "balance of probabilities" any reasonable person could see that Buddy was deceased, and in these cases, death certificates are issued without real proof that an individual has died.

The Social Security Department made it clear that it found little evidence that Buddy was really dead, but enough time had passed to declare him "legally" dead. Social Security cited the Jackson Police Department as knowing that The Baker Motel was well-known in the area as connected to the "underworld." Social Security admits that said motel denied anyone by the name of Buddy Heflin living at or even occupying a room at the motel for one night. Common sense tells me that the reason The Baker Motel and all who worked at it denied any association with Buddy was for the very reason that they did know what had happened to

Buddy Heflin, and that they all did know that he was dead.

I was now thirty-three-years old. Having Buddy's death on record would allow me to move on, have a small level of closure and receive the much-needed financial support from Social Security for Johnny and Ricky. Buddy had always wanted to provide for his sons even when he was too carried away with the nightlife to want to come home to us. I did not give an inch on this end; either Buddy would come home every night to his wife and sons, or the wife and the sons would move out. I might stay a week or two after he would make all of the right promises, and I still to this day believe that he was sincere in every attempt he made to bring us back home and keep his family together. What was it that was so tempting to him? Buddy would be so excited to have us all back together only to fall back to his old ways in a few weeks' time.

If he did fall victim to the lure quick money offered by organized crime, Buddy Heflin was not the only young man who did. Ever thirstier for the next dollar, and ever hungrier for the next level of power, nothing was too base, demeaning or illegal for the men at the top. With connections in all of the right places, horrendous crimes could be committed without expectation of the slightest bit of trouble or questioning from the police. That is why the power was so thrilling for these corrupt individuals; the main goal in their pathetic lives was to be able to not only threaten murder, but follow through, knowing that the crime could be committed with impunity. Only now with access to the internet to research those times in Mississippi do I fully understand the possibilities. In my twenties and thirties I knew about criminals, of course, but the idea that Buddy could be connected to the mob or any organization connected to organized crime did not occur to me until I was much older.

Finally on December 31, 1976, Judge Windels declared John Lloyd Heflin legally dead. Harold Barkley presented the findings, and the Judge signed it. The document afforded a small amount of closure but no much-needed financial support for my children. This news was devastating. Shortly after that, I received another debilitating blow, more whispers from Mississippi. The Department of Health, Education and Welfare had filed one more report requesting benefits from John Lloyd Heflin. Hannah Jo Allred was now claiming that her son who had been born after Buddy's disappearance was my husband's child. On the birth certificate she gave him my husband's last name.

I had never heard anything about this Michael Heflin. I had heard and knew for a fact that Buddy and Hannah Jo had been seeing each other after I had moved out and probably before, so I realized it was definitely possible for the two of them to have had a child. The startling part was that he existed. Did my two sons now have a half-brother? Children are not responsible for being brought into the world. A child does not ask to be born, and once he or she is born, those parents should treasure every minute of the blessing that is this precious little life.

We can sometimes think that more money to afford a bigger house or more toys or more opportunities is the answer. Time with the children helping them to grow in a safe place where they are loved is what matters. They need to be bathed, fed, clothed and should feel safe at night as they go to sleep. Their young futures can only begin to take shape if these things are in place. Furthermore, my personal belief is that children should be taught that there is a just God who governs the world and who loves us all. Whether the child is a Jew being taught from the Torah, a Muslim being taught from the Koran, or a Christian being taught from the Bible, growing up knowing that God is omniscient and omnipresent provides comfort when we are denied answers in this life. This may sound simple-minded, but is not the Truth usually very simple? Why not look for ways that make us all similar rather than focus on the things that make us different? If in fact this son is Buddy's, I trust and am hopeful that he receives the same help that my boys do.

The money from Social Security more than anything represents the acknowledgment that my sons grew up without their father. Years later in 1978 when Social Security granted Johnny and Ricky benefits beginning with the year Judge Windels declared Buddy legally dead, Johnny was fifteen and Ricky was thirteen. Benefits are provided up to the age of eighteen. What I do not understand is that Social Security deemed it appropriate to allocate one-third of the benefits due to my sons to Michael Heflin. This child was innocent, of course, and I wanted him to have all that he is entitled to receive from his father; it is very possible that he is my husband's son with another woman. But, does that possible truth warrant Social Security's decision to divide my sons' benefits by three? I had never known about Michael Heflin up to this point though, so to have their money divided by three without any advance notice and to learn about this child on a document from Social Security was naturally unexpected. To this day I still have no information regarding the whereabouts of Michael Heflin.

As far as Social Security goes, as of April 2013 when my niece and I drove to Starkville, the MFBI agents have begun the process to subpoena all of the records regarding Buddy Heflin. The Social Security Department is being asked to review the documents about Buddy Heflin and make sure the proper steps were taken all those years ago.

CHAPTER 19
Chicago 1977
Goes by Fast – Life in Chicago

IT WAS NOW 1977 AND JOHNNY was finishing high school at East Aurora High School in Chicago. Buddy had been missing almost ten years. Like most mothers, I could not believe how the years had passed by so quickly. I was so proud of both boys. All their lives they would pray for their daddy, and it never failed to break my heart when one of them and then the other would ask where their daddy was. The deep pain of Buddy's absence lived with us like some uninvited guest who refused to go home. The pain of not knowing is unwelcome, not Buddy himself. Buddy's loved ones want an ending, an explanation, a closing to the door of this mystery. Some doors close quickly, some more slowly and some doors never close . . . such is the mystery of my husband and my children's father. In this way, Buddy's absence has a physical presence that longs to be released from this world like the pages of an unfinished book left on a park bench whispering alone as they relent to the power of the wind.

At this point in the late 70s though, the boys were getting older and understood that I did not have any answers. Johnny earned his high school diploma, and Ricky followed two years behind his older brother. Except in this case, Ricky left his senior year of high school to see what the world could offer. He was anxious to get moving on with his life and away from school as most seniors are. Ricky was ready to start working so that he could start receiving a paycheck.

Fortunately, he saw fairly quickly that completing his education was a crucial step in the path to making a living and providing for a family, and he returned to school. His return was documented in *The Chicago Tribune*. My sister's husband who lived in Alabama was the one to see the article. Johnny and Ricky's Uncle Bill had always tried to advise them with what was the best route to take since their father had been gone for so much of their lives. Uncle Bill lived far away, but somehow the connection managed to grow, and the boys knew that their aunts and uncles believed in them. Family is still important to us; we know that whatever we encounter, we can count on our family to care for us and show us the right way. They can expect the same from us.

The reporter from *The Chicago Tribune* interviewed Ricky and other students, and their return to high school and the fact that they were welcomed without question to come back and graduate was documented in the article. Both of my boys worked hard and embraced their futures whole-heartedly. The three of us have always worked and appreciated the opportunities we have had in all of our endeavors. I am fortunate to have been able to provide for my children by working and not having to rely on the government for assistance. My work ethic and survival instincts are intact, and I am grateful that my sons understand that as well.

Not long after both of my sons had graduated from high school, I met a man at work, and we started to date. He had never been married, nor did he have any children. I felt that he would be a good role model for my sons because I knew him to be a gentleman and a very kind person. He was good-natured, gracious and straight forward with the boys and me. I felt blessed to have met him. Buddy had been missing at this point for almost ten years. The three of us were still in touch with Buddy's family in Mississippi, but Chicago was home for us now. When the man from work asked me to marry him, I decided to say, "Yes." We were married for only a couple of years when things started to unravel. He questioned my decisions about John and Rick, and then, of course, there was tension in the house. When the four of us were all together, none of us were comfortable. My husband wanted me all to himself, and although I understood his feelings, my children always came first. It was time for us to part. The separation was simple and uncomplicated. He cared for me, but the boys are most important, my world, and I would allow no one to come between us. The boys and I had been through too much together for any man to expect me to be able to make him top priority, and there was no way he could understand why.

The three of us were a family living in Chicago, but we also knew that we had family in different states that cared about us and knew that Johnny and Ricky had grown up without ever knowing what happened to their dad. Their aunts and uncles, both my siblings and Buddy's family, kept in touch with us and invited us to visit anytime with open arms. I lost two of my brothers in the summer of 1980. Their deaths were only a few months apart. My brother Willie F died as a result of a terrible accident. He had retired from the Air Force after twenty years of service and had begun crop dusting in Clarksdale. That morning he had gone up but landed the plane because of trouble with the sprayers. As he checked the sprayer underneath the plane which was still running, the cotton poison discharged into his face. Blinded and disoriented with the poison, Willie F stood up and walked into the propeller. My son Johnny was the one who called to tell me about Willie F; I dropped to my knees and cried.

I have so many reasons to be proud of my family. My big brother Willie F was a wonderful husband and father. He was always laughing and loved more than anything to get together and talk. When his daughter was getting to the age to go to dances with her friends and boys were included, Willie F was known to show up and then, all of a sudden, she would spot him in the crowd watching her on the dance floor. Nothing could have been more mortifying to his daughter, of course, but she would later laugh herself. He loved his family, and they were all so close. Willie F was wounded during the Korean War and received a Purple Heart for bravery. We all knew him to have a heart of gold. He was only forty nine when he passed away.

My whole family headed to Clarksdale to attend his military funeral. He served his country during the Korean War and two tours of the Vietnam War. There were six of us, my brothers and sisters, left now, and we all had children of our own. I had been asking God why He let this happen. How could He let this happen?

At the funeral my thoughts were no longer about me but Willie F's wife and children. Dolly, my sister-in-law, was so strong. She and I are still very close, and even after 31 years, she never remarried. Dolly openly says that the man she married was the love of her life, and no one could replace him.

Our family was still getting over the shock of losing Willie F when my phone rang a few weeks later. This time it was Gene, my brother who lived in Dallas, Texas. He had had a heart attack. Only a short time before, I had been to visit him. Gene was a pilot, too. During my visit he took me up in his plane for a ride and talked about all the things going on in our lives and how devastating Willie F's passing was. When it was time for me to leave, Gene did not want me to go, but I had to get back to Chicago and my job. We had had so much fun, and Gene continued to wave at me until I was out of sight. Perhaps he knew the end was near for him. I will never forget the smile on his face as he waved, and the plane taxied away. I still see him standing in the window as I left. That would be the last time I would see my brother. Gene had rheumatic fever as a child and had a bad heart valve as a result.

My brother Ray died a few months ago in 2013 after suffering a heart attack; he was eighty. I have lost three brothers, Willie F, Ray and Gene, and cherish the time I still have with my brother Leon and two sisters, Margie and Lena.

Part III:

Chasing shadows

CHAPTER 20
Huntsville 2003
Back to the South

MY SISTER LENA AND HER husband Bill lived in Huntsville, Alabama. She and her family moved to Huntsville, "The Rocket City," in the late '50s. After Bill graduated from high school up North, he moved to Mississippi to attend Mississippi State University. That is how the two of them met. Bill was an engineer and got a job at Redstone Arsenal. They built a life in Huntsville and remain there even to this day. Bill passed away in 2006, but his wife Lena and their three children who now have children of their own live in close proximity to each other. It had been so long since I had lived in the South.

I built a life with Johnny and Ricky in Chicago and now both of them have made their own lives and started families of their own after they graduated and moved on. I had mentioned to the boys that I would like to move closer to Lena because Bill's health had started to decline. For the forty years Lena had lived in Huntsville, the boys and I had visited often. Johnny and Ricky loved spending time with their Uncle Bill.

As adults the boys would visit, and Bill would take his son and two nephews deep-sea fishing, almost an annual tradition.

The opportunity for me to take an early retirement from Borg Seal Master Bearings came along, and I packed up and moved to Huntsville in January of 2003. I was torn between leaving the life I created in Chicago and the life I had left behind in Mississippi. I wanted to search and find out who I was and make a new life for myself.

Lena helped me find a condominium in the historic district of Huntsville known by the locals as "Five Points." To stay busy and occupy my time, Lena asked around where she shopped to see if anyone was hiring. Star Market Grocery was within walking distance of my new home, and they were looking for a cashier to replace a longtime employee who was retiring.

Lena and I went to the grocery store, and I met TJ, the store manager. He walked with me across the store to introduce me to the owner who was working in the pharmacy. The manager and I maneuvered our way up to the front counter through the ceiling-high stacks of over-the-counter medicines. TJ threw up his hand to a young gentleman with a big smile and red hair. TJ projected his voice with a big sigh of relief and said, "Darden, I have found the one we've been looking for. Meet Ethel Heflin." I had just become a member of the "Star" family.

Darden, wasting no time, said, "When do you start?"

And I replied, "Where's the register?" I knew this

was the place for me.

Everyone seemed so nice and welcomed me whole-heartedly even with my strong northern accent. Even though Huntsville is a fairly big city, it has a very small-town feel. Working at this grocery store, I felt as if I had befriended the whole town. People wanted to know where I was from and what had brought me here. It was a long time before I mentioned anything about my missing husband.

As I formed close relationships with the employees and customers, I was happily free to do all of the things that I had always wanted to do. I love to cook, and the staff loves to eat. The customers would come in and ask me if I had a recipe for a dish, and I would bring it in the next day so that they could buy the ingredients for that special dish right off the shelves. I often got requests for my coconut cake and sweet potato pie. I missed my boys, but the friendly people in my new hometown made a big difference.

On weekends Lena, Bill and I would take trips to Atlanta, Nashville, and Birmingham. Lena and I would shop while Bill waited for us to get hungry, and then we would all go eat and take a break before more shopping. Bill would drive us back home, and it was time to prepare for another work week at Star Market. The customers who come in to shop at Star Market are regulars. Seeing so many of them so frequently, if not daily, friendships developed, and they began to share their lives with me. I began to treasure my relationships with family and friends more than ever before. My life was finally mine, and I felt that I was finally in control of it. I thought of Buddy all of the time, but after filing the missing person's report all of those years ago, and the police ending the investigation so soon after, no one seemed to know anything. In small towns like Huntsville and Clarksdale, people talk up to the point of being intrusive and downright nosey sometimes. Everyone seems to be connected to everyone else in some way or another, so I never understood how Buddy's disappearance from Jackson could stay such a mystery. The ease of communication in a small town makes it almost impossible to keep a secret. I never let go of the idea that someone did know, maybe even police officers, but kept any information about Buddy undisclosed. For what reason, I am not sure.

One of the regular customers at Star Market is an attorney whose name is Chuck Brasher. He comes in almost every morning, and we make small talk. One day he looked at me and said, "You just do not look like an Ethel to me." I laughed out loud at his candid way of saying exactly what I had been thinking all of my life. Changing my name had crossed my mind, but it would just be a passing thought. My parents had given me this name, but I knew what he meant. I did not feel like an Ethel either. The next time he came in, I asked him what it would take to legally change my name and what it would cost.

The search to choose my new name began. I was so excited, but most people were probably thinking I was out of my mind or that changing my name was a silly thing to do. Those closest to me though knew I was sincere. Johnny and Ricky were amazed that I was prepared to make such a change after being "Ethel" for over 50 years. I really was ready, so I decided I was going to be Alexis Breanna Heflin. It suited me. I began to hear, "Hey, Alexis!" at work all the time. I appreciated their friendships, and their acceptance of my decision to change my name made me feel like I belonged.

Being tied to the memories of Buddy Heflin and his mysterious disappearance is a part of who I am, too. I kept these thoughts to myself most of the time. But the thoughts are with me all of the time. I love walking into work and seeing all the employees at the small neighborhood spot. I know that I am contributing and that my work is appreciated and valued. It is nice to hear when you are not at work that the customers want to know where you are and if you are okay. Buddy Heflin wanted the same thing. We all do. I had begun to look at life in a new light, but the shadows of the past started to grow larger and larger.

CHAPTER 21
Huntsville 2004
Decision to Write

THE NOTION OF WRITING a book hit home a few years earlier in 2004. I had given my attorney Peter Grometer who had helped me out in Chicago a call. He was the attorney who I contacted to help me have Buddy declared "legally" dead. He was now a retired judge in the court system in Chicago. He expressed disbelief that all of this had taken place and no one seemed to be investigating further, but he was unable to investigate anything on his end because he was retired. He listened as I told him that Earl Burch's wife was still alive, and living in Mississippi. She was with her husband when he committed suicide in their home. Earl had decided to shoot himself in the head shortly after Buddy disappeared. He had been with Buddy the last time he was seen.

I tried to talk with Earl Burch's wife about this myself, but she did not under any circumstances want to talk with me, and after she hung up on me, she never accepted another one of my calls. Why have the investigators not talked with her? They could reassure her that she would be safe. I feel certain that is why she will not talk even after all of these years. Her family has had to live in fear and with the knowledge that this husband and father had killed himself. I do not believe that this family or my family deserves any of this. If there are answers, let them be known, and let us find out. If so many people have been intimidated and made to live in fear, we can do something about it. We live in the 21st century, and the United States is not a third-world country or a dictatorship. People can be brought to justice. At this point, no one even needs to be punished. Could they be promised that no criminal charges would be filed if someone would have the courage to come forward with any information after all of these years? The idea crosses my mind, but I have no reason to think that anyone is in the Witness Protection Program.

Herein lies the reason for writing this book. At the end of my conversation with Judge Grometer, he unclosed his eyes after a minute, focused them on mine and did his best to articulate what his face expressed. He had never heard of a case like this, and suggested that I organize the facts and go public. I knew that if I were able to present what information we had and make it available for people to read, there would be a chance that someone would come forward. In any case, there was hope. People should not vanish under suspicious circumstances without someone documenting the evidence and pursuing the reason. Perhaps someone would see the book, read it and decide to come forward with information that can shed light on the missing pieces. I just kept thinking that I had too many unanswered questions to even start detailing my story for anyone to read. The thought that Buddy deserved to have his story told became a constant in my life. Whoever was responsible should be held accountable. The FBI confirms that anyone with information can come forward and remain anonymous. I am offering a reward for information that proves credible and leads to answers to Buddy's disappearance.

During the time between phone calls over the past couple of years living in Huntsville, Alabama, I started sharing my life with my co-workers. Each person listens intently as I am asked to talk about it again and again. No one ever indicates it, but I did wonder if anyone really believed me. I receive so much support from my co-workers, and I have asked from time to time what they thought about my writing it down. Gerald, in particular, is my side kick at the store; he is a few years older than I am and is so sweet and kind-hearted. We call ourselves "the dynamic duo" of the grocery store. I check the customers out, and Gerald bags the groceries and helps the customers unload them in their cars. He is always back in time to assist the next customer, and we continue working side by side, eight hours a day, five times a week. I can trust Gerald to tell me the truth, and I have been able to discuss the specifics of Buddy's case with him and see what he thinks.

Time and time again Gerald would insist, "Alexis — write it down!"

My manager over the years Mike has worked at Star Market since he was a teenager and is now in his early thirties. He laughs and says that his car only knows how to drive to Star Market. He encourages me to write the story, too. So does the butcher Robert and the pharmacy technician Stephanie. So many people stop by my register for an update on the case. Even the owner Darden Heritage finds time in his schedule to encourage me to get busy on Buddy's book. My Star Market family feels that if I could get the courage to start writing, it would help me process my feelings and perhaps remember things I have forgotten. People commented that no one's disappearance should go uninvestigated. Like in all companies, employees come and go, but I have invested a lot of myself into these people, and the relationships have helped me to make the decision to begin. I know they want me to succeed with my search for answers.

In early 2009, I was behind the register when I saw Darden in the corner of my eye smiling and talking with two other men. One was the new general manager Lonnie whom Darden had hired giving Darden more time to spend developing new business strategies, and more importantly, more time to spend with his four-year-old twin girls. The three men walked around the store stopping to discuss the others' opinions and ideas, and then I saw them head to the back of the store to Darden's office. Of course, like any "family," we were all very curious about the strangers.

I was making small talk with a customer as I rang up the groceries when I noticed the gentleman stranger observing me. After the customer walked out of the store, he looked at me and said, "I sure do like your store." I proudly replied, "Thanks," like it was my store because the employees at Star do feel a strong personal connection as if it is our store, too. Huntsville is a big city, but this particular area called "Five Points" has a very small-town feel.

The man reached over to shake my hand and introduced himself as Tom Feltenstein; he is the founder of the Neighborhood Marketing Academy and the author of many books. I found that out later.

It was very cold in Huntsville that day, and the first thing I noticed about him was that he was not wearing any socks. We talked for a few minutes, and then I just could not help asking him where his socks were. He chuckled and said, "Well, it was not cold where I was this morning." His speaking engagements have him traveling quite a bit.

After his meeting with Darden, he once again came back to my register. He was getting ready to leave, but he told me that because he was to be working with Darden on a new business venture, he would be back and see me again. When I asked him about the new project, he told me that it was still a secret. I responded and told him that I might be writing a book about a mysterious secret in my life. Little did I know that I was speaking to a marketing strategist, motivational speaker, entrepreneur as well as an author of five books of his own! He paused and wanted to know more about my book. What an unexpected experience! As the words were coming out of my mouth, I could see his mind taking it all in. He looked at me and said, "Make it happen!" His face lit up with genuine enthusiasm and went on to say, "I'll help you."

This was just what I needed to hear. We had several more conversations on the phone, and he gave me the information so that I could connect with a book agency in Boston. My journey to write the story for Buddy Heflin began on that February day.

For a year I worked to get facts from so long ago together, and the more I would write, the more it seemed that new evidence would surface which sent the book in all different directions. The various versions over the years have changed, but the motivation behind writing this book has always remained the same.

CHAPTER 22
Huntsville 2010
The Call from Gail Wofford

I HAD CREATED A NEW LIFE and was very content. I lived in Chicago from 1967-2003, and I was now living in Huntsville. My work at Star Market was demanding because the store stays busy from morning to night, but working for Darden is worth it. He works very hard and appreciates his employees. So, I have a great place to work, and I am able to see my family all the time. I talk with my boys on the phone several times a week and make frequent trips to see them and their families. I was spending quite a bit of time with Lena and Bill before he passed in 2006. There is never any real closure or peace of mind for people who lose someone they love to violence, and I have always felt that Buddy's life was taken from him by people who were involved in criminal activities. I did not know how to pursue what I thought were negligent investigations into what happened to Buddy, but I do know that more could have been done. I do know that either the police officers in Starkville chose not to follow the leads because they were lazy and did not care or because they were involved and did not want to go to jail themselves.

I would sit at home some evenings wondering how our lives would have been different if Buddy had not vanished. John and Rick would have grown up with their father. I would think about where we might be living. The boys had their father's mannerisms and looks. There was no denying they were Buddy's children. I now have a beautiful granddaughter named Emily Ann, and she, too, resembles Buddy. They all have his olive skin, thick eyelashes and beautiful smile. What kind of grandfather would Buddy have been? Where was he? What kind of trouble had he gotten himself into? I wonder if Buddy and I would have reconciled and had the united family I always dreamed about. He might have grown up a little, as most men in their late twenties do, and he and I would have one of those long-lasting marriages and grow old together.

One afternoon in the spring of 2010 after I had come home from work, my cell phone rang. It was Buddy's sister on the other end. She asked me if I were sitting down because she had information about Buddy. I broke out in a cold sweat and felt a rush of adrenaline that made me dizzy. I was silent for a minute, and then I heard her ask me if I were still there. I said, "Yes. Please tell me what happened."

Buddy's best friend growing up was a girl named Gail Wofford. They had gone all the way through school together and lived close by on the same street. She had recently had a heart attack which really scared her, and she began thinking about the people in her life whom she had really cared about the most. Buddy Heflin had been one of those friends to her, and Gail had been devastated when he vanished. But she had also been very afraid. Gail was ready to talk about the secrets she had been keeping for forty-one years. She had information to share and was no longer scared to tell what she knew. None of us ever understood why Gail moved away from home right after Buddy disappeared; we all knew what good friends they were. That fact is that she moved to Georgia because she was afraid for her own life. Buddy had a girlfriend named Hannah Jo, and she, too, disappeared only to resurface years later trying to get a new driver's license under a different name. I would not have been concerned about Hannah Jo because I did not know her. However, we were all concerned about Gail because she was such a close friend.

I have to wonder if Hannah Jo were afraid as well. The story Gail tells now sounds very much like testimony from witnesses who barely escaped with their lives after getting involved with the notorious Dixie Mafia. We do not know for certain, but present-day reports validate the existence of this group of criminals also known as the Southern Mafia. The investigators are now following leads to determine if there is concrete evidence that Buddy died because he refused to follow any more orders from men in organized crime.

Months before Buddy's disappearance in 1969, Gail received a call at work from him. He was panicked and asked her to please meet with him. Gail had worked third shift at the restaurant, so even though it was early in the morning, she was ready to go home and get some sleep. Gail knew him well enough to know that something bad had happened or Buddy would not have been begging and insisting with her to talk to him. Gail says that when Buddy got to the parking lot where she was waiting, his appearance was startling. He had not shaved his face, and he was shaking. Buddy had been known to drink too much alcohol but never first thing in the morning. So Gail was not completely sure that he had been not been drinking, but she soon learned that his trembling was caused by fear. He had to tell her something, and she listened.

Buddy confided in Gail that he had gotten involved with some people who were now threatening his life. He begged her to ride with him to a certain house because he was instructed to meet with two people named Keith and Doris Warren who lived there. Buddy said that if he talked with them and explained himself, they might understand and let him walk away from the situation or give him another chance. Gail was really concerned after hearing all of this because Buddy was a childhood friend, and she had never before seen him like this.

Once they got to the house and knocked on the door, Buddy took a deep breath and waited for someone to answer the door. The door jerked opened, and a voice told Gail where to sit and that she was to wait. Gail recognized this woman and knew she was Doris Warren. Gail watched Buddy as he walked to a back room, and then the woman slammed the door behind them so that Gail could not hear exactly what was being said. She could hear Buddy's voice pleading with these people. The voices that spoke back were angry and loud.

When Buddy came out of the room, Gail could see that he was terrified and crying. He was twenty-five-years old and so was Gail, but at that moment she felt like they were little kids again. She could not wait to get out of that place and away from that neighborhood. Gail got in the driver's seat and waited for Buddy to tell her what in the world was going on. Buddy continued to cry and tremble refusing to tell her because if he did, her life would be in danger, too.

The voices in the house had made that very clear to Buddy. He let her know: "My life isn't worth a plug nickel, and yours won't be either if I tell you everything." What he did tell her was enough to scare this young lady so badly that she left almost immediately and would not tell anyone why. Buddy told Gail that the couple had offered him a lot of money if he would agree to do a "one-time deal." He went on to tell her that something happened that was not supposed to happen, and he saw something that he was not supposed to see.

Gail wanted to help Buddy to get out of this trouble, so she took Buddy to see Gail's father who tried his best to get Buddy to go to the police; he just kept repeating that they had promised him that if he went to the authorities, they would kill his whole family. The motto of the Dixie Mafia is: "THOU SHALT NOT SNITCH TO THE COPS." From what I understand, this organization works within and without of the prison system, and thrived like cockroaches in the small towns of Jackson, Starkville, and Gulfport, Mississippi, in the 1960s. I have done research on the Internet trying to come up with possible reasons that Buddy would have been murdered without ever knowing why. With no information after all of these years, I have considered all possible reasons for why he is gone.

So, Gail had remained quiet about what she knew until forty years later. After her heart attack, she thought she was going to die, and it now means so much to her that she do all she can to find an answer, and she has. Thankfully, she has recovered from the heart attack, and we are able to encourage and support each other as the detectives continue to search for answers. The couple from the house all of those years ago is still living in Mississippi. Keith and Doris Wilson are also known as Warren and Doris Floyd and have both served time in prison. The last time Buddy's sister ran in to "Doris" who was out running errands in Clarksdale, Doris told her that she had just taken a lie detector test, and that she had passed and had been cleared of suspicion by the police. I immediately called Alan Thompson of the MFBI and reported what she had said. This chance meeting between Buddy's sister and Doris was just a few months ago in June of 2013.

I do not know what to make of this except to say that I appreciate those investigators in Starkville, Mississippi, more than I can say. Something is being done just like they said it would be. During the past three months, the detectives have stayed in close contact with me. I have reviewed autopsy photos of one man for the slim chance that it might be Buddy. The man in the photos was not Buddy Heflin, but he was someone's brother or son. DNA tests have been done on my sons so that the information can be run through databases for matches to other claimed deceased. Lie detector tests have been given. The morning in April of 2013 when my niece and I left the police station where we had been discussing Buddy for three hours, I was about to leave when Lt. Kenneth Bailey stopped me and said, "Mrs. Heflin, I want to look you in the eyes, and make sure you know that I am going to do all I can to find out what happened to your husband."

Gail Wofford had called Buddy's mother right after he disappeared in 1969, but she would only say that he was gone but not how or why. She wanted to offer some comfort to Buddy's mother who had been like a second mother to her, but Gail did not dare say anything about what she knew. Gail was too scared to give any details. Buddy's father was understandably distraught because his son was missing, and there were only rumors and silence instead of answers. Buddy's father passed away within three months of Buddy's disappearance. Not knowing where your child is must be the loneliest place in the world. There were no answers only massive speculation that seemed to ebb and flow as the years went by. Because of Gail being courageous enough to come forth recently, we now have the names of others who Buddy told her were involved in the dangerous and deadly business that he had gotten himself entangled—in addition to Doris and Keith Warren, Buddy gave Gail the names of Red Davis, Hannah Jo Allred, Julius Davis and Earl Burch.

At this point in 2010, forty years after Buddy vanished, I knew that I needed to go back to Mississippi. When I hung up the phone, I called John and Rick to tell them what Gail Wofford was saying now. Our lives had once again been turned upside down because of the secret whisperings in Mississippi that refuse to be silenced. The boys and I believe that eventually the truth comes to light, no matter how embarrassing or disturbing that truth is. That being said, I am very aware that the strictest attention must be paid because as much as I want closure, I do not want anyone who is innocent to be forced to live under the cold and lonely judgment of suspicion.

CHAPTER 23
Jackson 2010
Back to Mississippi with
New Information for the FBI

JOHN AND RICK ARE NOW GROWN, and I can let my guard down a little. I started talking to them about details that I had never told them when they were little. I was afraid that after all of these years, I would not remember something important, so I started asking family members what they remembered; I wanted to know what they remembered and even suspected. I needed to be clear when I spoke with the police and make sure that my facts were straight. The boys wanted to go with me, but they had families of their own and responsibilities. I needed to see what was really going on before giving them more details.

I called Jimmy Bryant, Buddy's nephew, to see if he would mind taking me to the police station to meet with the investigators. Jimmy was so supportive and said that he could not wait to see me again after all these years. I have always stayed in touch with Buddy's family because I could feel that they were as anxious as I was to find out what happened to their uncle, son and brother. Jimmy was the one who went to The Baker Motel, the last place Buddy was living, to see his uncle. Buddy had disappeared at that point, and Jimmy asked the clerk at the front desk to let him in Buddy's room. The room had been completely trashed. The doors and drawers were all open, and Buddy's belongings were strewn throughout the room. We all knew Buddy to be extremely particular about his clothes and liked everything to be organized and in its place; he liked his clothes pressed and starched, his bed made, and he did not like clutter. This room had been destroyed by someone either looking for something specific, or because there had been a fight or some struggle. That was forty years ago. Right before Buddy disappeared without a trace, Buddy had asked Jimmy to come visit him at the motel where he had been living. That was Christmas of 1968. Jimmy was not able to go see his uncle in time. By the time Jimmy headed to The Baker Motel, Buddy was missing. Everyone who knew Buddy was extremely concerned because no one had any answers. Family and friends were trying to reassure Buddy's mother that he would be found. Jimmy promised to help find him, but Jimmy left the hotel more concerned than ever after seeing his room. He contacted Deputy Harpole expecting immediate results, but Jimmy waited and was never contacted.

Now I was seeing Jimmy for the first time in thirty-three years when I had met with him in Mississippi at the Social Security Office trying to see if the boys and I qualified for any benefits. The last time I had seen him would have been in 1970, one year after Buddy stopped contacting anyone. When I crossed the Mississippi line this time, my heart rate began to beat faster. I just wanted to find out the truth no matter what that truth would be. The streets were still familiar to me. Some of the buildings had new businesses in them, but my mind would think back to what had been there the last time I was in town. The reality is that we all want and need to know the truth about the people we love as much as we dread finding it out. My heart and my mind were both racing as I drove the streets remembering all the hurt, betrayal and lies that caused me to leave Buddy for the last time and move back to Chicago back in April of 1968, just months before he vanished. I was relieved when I finally got closer to Jimmy's house and pulled into the old familiar driveway. My hands did not want to let go of the grip I had on the steering wheel. I lifted each hand and opened the car door slowly. I looked up to see an older version of the young Jimmy I used to see all the time. His smile was just as warm as it used to be. He gave me a hug and told me that I had not changed a bit.

Jimmy was from such a good family who stayed out of trouble, valued education and respected and valued this country, and his brother Kenny and beautiful little sister Suree are still living. Jimmy passed away in 2011 after losing the battle to heart and lung disease. Jimmy's mother Francis Hancock was Buddy's sister. The day Jimmy accompanied me to the Jackson Police Department I could tell that he was a very sick man. He did not live but a few months after this. His heart was in bad shape, and Jimmy was on oxygen.

What a wonderful friend he was to me! I hope he knows how much I appreciated him. It was so hot outside, and I did not want Jimmy to have to get out in the brutal heat, and I wanted him to stay home: "I am going to go with you. I'll be alright. I will probably not live too much longer, and I am grateful for the chance to be able to help you find out about my uncle if I can." I realized that he was determined to go with me, and so I did not say another word about it.

Jimmy and I sat back down after I walked a bit to stretch my legs, and we started talking over the notes each of us had jotted down as we drank a couple of sweet teas. The news that Gail Wofford shared with Buddy's other sister Annie Belle had been told to us so recently. The recent events were difficult to grasp, and it took all of us talking and keeping notes to make sure that we were ready to make these statements to the police and investigators. The next morning I called John and Rick who were expecting a phone call as soon as I left the police department. The night before I barely closed my eyes it seemed, and it was time to wake up. I closed my cell phone when Jimmy pulled up and waited for me to get in his car. As we got closer to the dark brick of the police station, I realized that it looked exactly the same as it had forty-one years ago when the missing person's report was filed for Buddy.

After Jimmy parallel parked the car, and I put a quarter in the meter, we entered the double doors of the police station. We were headed for the Robbery and Homicide Division. I could barely feel my legs as the elevator door opened, and I stepped out onto the floors I had tread so long ago when I was only twenty three. I now had the wisdom of time, experience and hindsight, and I did my best to have every piece of paper conceivable that the investigators might ask for, but I was still so nervous. The fear that Buddy had been murdered by people so greedy for money and power and were able to escape justice all of these years never fails to overwhelm me no matter how many years pass by. Jimmy was nervous, too, but he was being strong to support me.

We walked up to a desk, and the receptionist told us to have a seat. When we explained that we had evidence about a cold case that had just been reopened, she realized that we were on the wrong floor in the wrong department. She left us for a few minutes and returned with a gentleman by the name of Sergeant Eric T. Smith, Sr. He said, "Mrs. Heflin, would you mind coming to my office so you can brief me about why you are here?"

I replied trying to smile and be respectful, "I would have been disappointed if you didn't want to know why I have driven from Alabama to speak with you. I need answers to decades of questions."

Sgt. Smith nodded in a very slow and deliberate way and said, "Let's see what we can do."

Jimmy sat with me as I told the Sergeant the events leading up to his parents filing a missing person's report in 1969. I gave a detailed report of all the new information I had learned over the years up until the most recent news from Gail Wofford. I showed him all of the paperwork that I had and a list of names. Sgt. Smith started researching the people of interest on his computer. As he would type in the names and dates, a strange look appeared on his face. After a while he looked up from his computer screen, picked up the phone and called another office. Jimmy and I were then led upstairs to the FBI office.

I guess my face turned pale because he quickly stated that what we needed could not be supplied by his department. The necessary serious and professional demeanors of investigators and detectives can be very intimidating. I understand that it is necessary in order for them to do their jobs, but the information they provide always seems to be just the bare minimum, and it has never gotten easier for me to deal with. Sgt. Smith went as far as the elevators with Jimmy and me. The doors closed, and we pushed the button for Level 3 — The Federal Bureau of Investigations in Mississippi.

As soon as the doors opened, an eager Captain Raymond Delk greeted us. The office itself held five different stations each with a desk and computer and investigator. He showed us to his station where we were seated. Once again I relived the events of the past and the recent evidence that had brought me there that day. Captain Delk asked numerous questions about the cold case, and he, too, started searching files on his computer. He would ask me to spell the names again, and he would ask me if I were sure about the dates. I felt that I was sure, because I had worked so hard to have everything in line before we came. I became aware of the agents at the other desks, and it seemed as if everyone were listening and working on the files, and then I noticed mirrors that seemed to be watching me. This experience was probably due to the many movies and TV shows I have seen where possible suspects were watched by people out of plain sight.

Captain Delk finally took his eyes away from the computer screen and locked them on me. He said that in all the years, he had never seen so many files on this many people that had just disappeared from an FBI database and the Police Department of Jackson, Mississippi. What was it that he was saying to me?

What could he possibly mean? Not expecting to hear anything like this, I tried to remain calm and offer more information. I said that I knew that Buddy had worked with Earl Burch at the Kroger in Jackson. Jimmy Bryant had worked with Julius Davis driving trucks for the same company, and we told Raymond Delk the story about the time Julius, not knowing that Jimmy was Buddy's nephew, blurted out, "That ol' Buddy Heflin? Why they killed his a--!"

Jimmy said, "Buddy Heflin was my uncle," and, Julius was not about to say one more word. Jimmy and I tried to think of more to tell.

I felt the need to do something more. I wanted to tell him that I could call someone who knew someone who knew of Doris Warren, Keith Warren, Red Davis, Julius Davis--Captain Delk expressed disbelief and curiosity, but I could tell that he had no intentions of letting me in on what he was thinking. Perhaps he knew more about the goings on and connections among the names than I did. That thought was unnerving, but it gave me hope.

He finally backed away from the desk, stood up and said that he would need some more time to make calls, but that he was confident he had enough information to re-open the case and start gathering information for a Grand Jury. I could not believe what he had just said, "A Grand Jury!" Nothing ever came of the Grand Jury; the cold case was deemed "active," but Raymond Delk retired not long after this, and I cannot help but think this was very strange. He had convinced me that I could trust him.

Usually a criminal case gets started with a police arrest report. The prosecutor then decides what criminal charges to file, if any. To my knowledge, there had been no arrests, and Buddy's body had never been found; therefore, no autopsy or coroner's report and no crime scene. How often is this the case? What Captain Delk must have meant is that he believed enough in the evidence and testimony that had not disappeared from the FBI database, to present the information to Grand Jurors who do not choose guilt, but decide if the case has probable cause to go to trial. Did he think that charges might possibly be filed against the police department for negligence? Had the police department in 1969 been negligent? Of course, I now had more questions than I did before I drove back to Mississippi. The one constant was that Buddy Heflin deserves a concerted effort on the part of the Mississippi officials and all of us who knew him to find out what happened to him!

Captain Delk said that Jimmy and I could go home and that he would be in touch. I did not like this at all. I was getting more questions, not any answers. I had more questions and no answers. This same thought raced through my mind, and I was not even aware of the elevator ride down or the walk outside to the car until Jimmy reached out and patted me on the back. He starting talking and reassuring me that he felt that Raymond Delk was going to get to the bottom of the missing files and find out how these people were connected and who may have been involved.

When I called John and Rick, they could not believe that all of the files had disappeared. I still could not believe it myself. Should someone file a "missing" missing person's report? I wanted to be able to tell my sons and the rest of my family something else. My sons wanted to know how I was holding up. It had been a long day, and my throat hurt from talking so much. I had been speaking to so many people preparing for the meeting with the detectives; I wanted to have everything in order so that no more time was wasted. I did not want any delay for the investigation to be because I had not done my homework.

I headed back to Huntsville to once again wait for the phone to ring. Every time my cell phone would ring, my heart would race. A week later I did finally receive a call from a man who said his name was Clay. He stated that Captain Delk had handed the investigation over to him in Louisville, Mississippi. He informed me that he was a private investigator. I did not understand why this case would need to go outside the city of Jackson to a private investigator. I did not, however, express this to Clay; instead, I listened as he left a number for me to call and told me to contact him if I could think of anything else after our initial telephone interview. He let me know that he would be investigating the events and setting up interviews.

I received a letter from Raymond Delk dated June 10, 2010, confirming that indeed the cold case of John Lloyd Heflin who came up missing in January of 1969 and had not been seen since, has now become an "active" cold case. Little did I know or could I have imagined that the act of re-opening the case would bring what seemed to be more "cover-up," closed interviews with information I would not be privileged to because the case was "active" once again.

Clay and I did touch base monthly about what he was doing. After several months of this, I nicknamed him "my mystery man." I did not tell him or anyone that he had a nickname but kept it to myself. Unfortunately, and very frustrating, Clay would inevitably provide the same answer: "I do not have any new information leading to any answers to your questions." Clay claimed to have spoken with the names on the list provided by Gail Wofford. He had spoken with Doris and Keith Warren, and they said that they did not remember anything about this case. That has been hard for me to believe because Buddy had gone to school with both Doris and Keith. The three of them had all gone to school with Dolf Bryant who was Deputy Sheriff in Jackson from 2009-2011. He had promised me that he would investigate the case, but the evidence shows that Deputy Sheriff Dolf Bryant did nothing. I do not see how this small town managed to keep someone's mysterious disappearance from reaching everyone in that community much less reach the ears someone's former classmate who is the same age.

Each time Clay called, I gave him the information he requested; I did not mind repeating myself time after time. I knew he was busy with so many other cases and not just mine. Many times I provided the same information as I had the previous time. Clay and I would talk while he was making notes, investigating and interviewing, locating suspects and family members, but he had to remind me that because it was an "active" case, he could not answer most of my questions about what he was learning, especially over the phone. I tried my best to understand and respect his responsibility to all of the cases he was working on. I made every effort to make myself available to each and every call, but I cannot be on the phone at my job when there are customers ready to pay for their groceries, so I did miss a few calls.

I did learn from Clay that Hannah Jo had resurfaced in Jackson two years prior in 2008. She had been trying to get a driver's license with falsified records, and when that failed, she had disappeared once again. When I left Buddy in 1967 and moved to Chicago, Hannah Jo was part of the reason. We got married in 1961, and I was pregnant with Little John by 1963. Looking back Buddy must have already begun on the path that led to getting himself into trouble about two years later. That must have been when the bad connections began. What I knew right then was that I had two children to take care of, and my husband seemed to stay away from home more and more often. I would move out and then move back in, but I left for good in 1967. Buddy had been seeing Hannah Jo for some time even though we were still legally married. Hannah Jo was with Buddy during those late nights out at the bars and everywhere else, I suppose. I cannot be certain, but the reason for her disappearing seems to indicate that she knew something that put her life in danger. She knew the people that Buddy had befriended in Jackson better than I did.

Both Raymond Delk and Clay said they tried to find her but could not. I felt so strongly that she knew information that no one else did. From the research I had been doing myself, I found an obituary and learned that Hannah Jo Allred had died in Jackson in 2011 from cancer, so I wonder why no one could find her. I am suspicious that no one even looked for her. I had been giving names of anyone who could provide information. Deputy Harpole and later Captain Delk both claimed that she could not be found. I also found out from the obituary that she had a son whom she named Michael Heflin. This child with my husband's last name was born in January of 1969. I had been living in Chicago with the boys for two years by that time.

So that I could claim Social Security benefits for the boys, Buddy Heflin was declared legally dead in 1975 by a judge in Mississippi seven years after his disappearance New Year's Eve 1968. I never changed my last name because of my children, and even though Buddy and I were not living together when he disappeared, we had never divorced. I left him and moved to Chicago in 1967. Buddy had never married Hannah Jo. I had filed for Social Security Benefits in June of 1973 so that I could support my two sons, but I was denied any benefits because according to the report dated May 3, 1974, "Section 202 of the Social Security Act, as amended, provides under circumstances for payment of monthly insurance benefits to the survivors of an insured worker. The worker must however be a retirement beneficiary, a disability insurance beneficiary, or he must be deceased." The report goes on to say that there is "little concrete evidence as to what might have occurred to the worker. It appears that the worker had Thanksgiving Day dinner in 1968 at his mother's home at Starkville, Mississippi . . . Mrs. Willie Mae Holland (Buddy's sister) was the last of the family evidently who saw the worker. This was on New Year's Day of 1969."

The report goes on to cite when different family members had seen Buddy for the last time: "He was in the company of a 'Red Davis' who later was in Pardiman Prison, Mississippi." Earl Burch is mentioned as well and cited as saying via a sister of Buddy's that Earl called her on December 25, 1970, to inform her that Buddy's body had been thrown into the Mississippi River at Vicksburg six months prior. The report records the "missing" missing person's report as early as August 13, 1973, when Social Security checked at the Jackson Police Department. Accordingly, an arrest record was found that named "the worker" as being arrested for fighting and public intoxication "sometime" in 1969. I would think that an arrest record would be more specific than "sometime." So, I question Social Security mentioning this in the report, and I question the filing system at the Jackson Police Department.

The final finding was that John L. Heflin "had a very good reason for wishing to disappear" because there is evidence indicating he may have been engaged in criminal activities, that no one at the Baker's Motel remembered anyone having lived there by that name, and that, "The local enforcement agencies stated that this motel had connections with the underworld." I could not make this up myself; it is written on the document in black and white, so I moved on with my life with my two sons, and I did my best to raise them with the money I earned from working two jobs.

In addition to calls from Clay, one day I received a phone call from a man named Howard Miller. He told me that he was an attorney and needed to speak with me about getting ready to present evidence to a Grand Jury. He did not know when it would happen, but we had to prepare for it like it would be tomorrow. A Grand Jury for whom or what? I was still in the dark, but the phone calls gave me hope that we were getting close. I knew that there were more people out there who had information for the missing pieces. Three years later there has been no Grand Jury, and no one mentions having a Grand Jury trial anymore.

I finally got to meet Clay when my niece and I went back to Mississippi in April of 2013. I gained a new perspective and so much more respect after meeting him in person. He is a dedicated investigator and cares deeply about every case. I am fortunate that he is on my side. My niece and I were both somewhat skeptical as we made the drive, but she and I both were immensely impressed and extremely grateful.

Raymond Delk's documents cannot be found at this point, but he must have records from when I visited in 2010. Howard Miller may be the one who has the information. These two men can be questioned.

CHAPTER 24
2011-2013
Awaiting Grand Jury Trial

DURING ALL OF THE MONTHS since receiving the phone call from Buddy's sister telling me about what Gail Wofford wanted to share with us, I had received an actual hand-written letter from her, so I mailed a copy to Detective Delk, but time seemed to be moving in slow motion. I wanted time to speed up to the time when we had all the facts and the person or persons responsible found and named.

I was in constant contact with John and Rick trying to make sure they knew all that was developing. The boys had been my life and finally getting some closure would perhaps heal some feelings that they had carried inside their hearts and minds during their lives. I would worry about how these events in the past were affecting their lives in the present.

Growing up Johnny and Ricky got questioned often about their father. The boys and girls at their school would want to know, "Why don't you have a dad?" Neither of them could answer because they did not know either. Children would innocently ask, "How come you never get to go fishing or hunting with your dad? Did something happen to him? Did he die?" The boys would come home from school and tell me about this, and when I would see them so sad, it never failed to break my heart. We did have each other though, and we are very close; I have always been grateful for this. Children understand when a parent passes away or a mother and father divorce, but how could I explain that their father was just gone.

They do not like to talk about what may have happened to their father. They would like to know why so very little was ever done by the police to find out, but speculating about the hearsay and rumors is not something they are comfortable with. They look so much like Buddy, so sometimes I think that he is still around and with us because I can just look at them. They really question our justice system sometimes because the reality is that it works for some people, but not all people. That is just the way it is, and I realize that. At times they have mentioned taking over for me and trying themselves to pursue the leads because time can feel like it is running out. Even though they are now grown men, I still see two little boys wanting to pray every night for their dad to be safe and come back home.

If we could finally get this solved, the Social Security benefits for the seven years before Buddy was declared legally dead would be paid to us with interest for over forty years. There is also an insurance policy that would finally pay out. Perhaps the boys could use this money to make their lives a little better for themselves and their families. My most recent contact with Social Security indicated that if the case were to ever go before a Grand Jury, and the Judge were to make the decision with a definite determination, we would receive back pay for those seven years.

I survived without that money while raising my two sons, but the boys were without a father. Perhaps the money would make up for a little of the pain they endured. John and Rick never ask about what is happening with Social Security because they are not really concerned with getting any money. They have good work ethics and do not mind getting up every day and going to work. We have always been able to joke around about how our lives read like a good book, but like the case, the book never ends.

I would like most for my sons and myself to have an answer though, but sometimes it feels like that will never happen. I believe answers and the findings after the MFBI re-evaluates Social Security procedures will help heal the wounds of unanswered questions and not knowing. Our faith reassures us that there will definitely be a Judgment Day to come, and at that point, we will know the Truth. Thank goodness, for our faith in God: "Now we see but a poor reflection as in a mirror; then we shall see face to face. Now I know in part; then I shall know fully, even as I am fully known" (1 Corinthians 13: 12).

CHAPTER 25
2012
Potential for New Information To Surface

I KNOW THAT COLD CASES are not top priority with the over-burdened criminal justice system, but there had never been any closure for my sons, and with all of the new information coming to light, my hopes were high of finding out where Buddy had died and bringing those involved to justice. This had become my mission. I want so much to learn the details of what had become of Buddy for my boys and me. We all hope that someone would do the same for us if we mysteriously vanished without a trace. I had to become a part of the investigation of John "Buddy" Lloyd Heflin's case.

Earl Burch's family members are being interviewed as well as other people of interest. The cloud of suspicion that hangs over some of these people must surely be oppressive especially if they are innocent. Hannah Jo has died of cancer as of 2011, and the son that she named Michael Heflin is presumed to still be living. He could possibly have information.

A friend suggested that I contact *The Clarion Ledger* in Jackson, Mississippi, to spark some interest in the public about the upcoming book. The reporter who answered the phone was Therese Apel. After hearing the story, she stated that she could help. The newspaper posted a Facebook story about the case in September of 2012 so that people could read about it and see if anyone would come forward with information.

Thankfully so many people responded wanting to know more about the case. People are asking why more time was not put to finding evidence forty years ago? Readers want to know if there was a connection between the people involved with Buddy's disappearance and the police department. Had there been a cover-up? Corruption in our country's protection agencies threatens democracy itself, our national security. People officers are community members living in our neighborhoods whom we trust, but why would they have stopped searching all those years ago?

Thanksgiving of 2012 came, and I remember being so grateful for the blessings in my life. My family and I went on to celebrate Christmas as well. The year ended, and I realized that the book is a celebration of the short time I had with Buddy Heflin. It is also a celebration of everyone who has ever been a part of my life, but especially Buddy because the end to his short life is still a mystery.

Part IV:

Rest

for the

Weary

CHAPTER 26
My Childhood

Even so, Father: for so it seemed good in the sight

(Matthew 11:26)

DECEMBER 31, 1946, WAS THE coldest day I have ever known. When I was three, I was told that Mama was "with child," but after seven months of waiting for the baby, we tragically lost them both. We had that one last Christmas with her, and she died a few days later. The older children had found the Christmas presents in the attic, and all of the Christmas cookies. I was too young, of course, to remember, but we still tell the story of riding the tricycles and eating the cookies.

On the day she died, Mama had washed a load of clothes and needed Daddy to hang them out to dry. He was going to hang the clothes for her as soon as he finished the work he had to do in the barn for the animals. We had chickens and cows and a beautiful year-round garden. Evidently, Mama got impatient and decided to hang the clothes herself. She knew how busy Daddy was, and she, too, was used to being busy. She had seven children to take care of, and one more on the way. Somehow while doing the laundry, Mama lost her balance, slipped on the ice and fell down hard. Dr. Walker came to the house and told Mama to get and stay in bed until the baby came. She must have been hemorrhaging.

After several days with no change in her condition, Mama became so weak that she was finally taken to the hospital. When they told my father that she and the baby were gone, they say he collapsed against the hospital wall.

Her body was brought home, and she was in the living room next to the big picture window. A memory etched in my mind since I was three years old is being picked up to look into the casket where Mama lay silent and cold to give her a last kiss goodbye. For the funeral the girls were dressed in our Sunday dresses--hand-made lace dresses that my mother made--and the four boys wore pants with white shirts and blazers. Family and friends gathered together at Mount Moriah Cemetery where she is buried. She was 37 when she passed away. She loved going to school and had graduated from high school before she got married. She loved to play the piano, and my oldest brothers learned how to play by sitting next to Mama on the bench. She sang while she played the piano and grew up playing in church.

Mama had dark brown hair and according to my father, "eyes as blue as the Southern sky." Every Sunday my mother would dress my two older sisters and me in our special lace dresses that she had made, get the four boys and Daddy ready, and all of us would be together at church on time. I can still picture the church with bright red brick in our hometown of Union City, Tennessee. Once seated on the pew, we children knew to be quiet as mice during the sermon. If any one of us caused the least disturbance, we would see Mama's hat bobbing back and forth signaling her disapproval. I am so proud that when I look back, I know that my parents understood the value of family.

I have always looked up to my mother because she made a coconut cake to die for, kept an immaculate house, was a wonderful wife and the most beautiful woman I had ever seen.

There was so much love and comfort in our house when my mother was alive. We lived in a small red brick house with red shutters, and all of the rooms were furnished to suit her particular taste. The house was always clean, and everything was in its place. Mama was a good cook and a good housekeeper. I listen to my older brothers and sisters talk about her, and so some of their memories have become mine as well. The front porch swing was a favorite place for her on pretty days.

I remember that my brother Ray played the piano for Mama on those days before she died. She requested, "If I Could Hear My Mother Pray Again," and Ray played and sang the song over and over again. She was not getting any better lying in bed; in fact, she stopped eating and became weaker and weaker with every day that passed. I remember one of my mother's friends coming over to the house to check on her, but as hard as she tried to prepare food that Mama would eat, nothing piqued her appetite. The friend would peal oranges for Mama. I can still see that orange on Mama's nightstand. Even at very young ages God places certain things that remain in our memories all of our lives.

After my mother's death, my father went back to work at the saw mill from seven to five, seven days a week to put food on the table for the seven children.

Thinking back now, I hope the hard work gave him an escape from the reality of my mother's death. Because he was away at work so much, my siblings and I had to split up the chores. One of us would cook while someone else did the dishes; the rest cleaned. We played Rock Paper Scissors or drew straws sometimes to decide who did what. Even though I had family all around me, I always felt alone and abandoned without my mother. I envied other little girls when I saw them with their mothers at the grocery store or walking down the sidewalk in town. My brothers and sisters must have felt the same loss at school and on the ball fields.

The reminders of my mother in the little town of Union City were eventually too much for my father to bear. He moved us to Clarksdale, Mississippi, where I have most of my memories growing up. Had we stayed in Tennessee with my mother's family, my brothers and sisters would have been separated from each other and sent to live with different family members. There were seven of us, and they could not understand how my father was going to take care of all of us without my mother. I understand that Mama's family wanted the best for her children, but Daddy insisted that we would all stay together, and we did. He had overheard my mother's family discussing who would take which children. Not long after the funeral, we all left.

Daddy seemed much happier in Mississippi because he had the support of his family now. We children had not wanted to leave, but we had no way of comprehending Daddy's reasoning. A moving truck came, and he packed all of our clothes and a few personal belongings. He left most of the furniture, but he did bring some personal items of my mother's and kept them for a very long time.

Daddy was good to us. Maybe he was not able to take us all to church every Sunday like Mama did, but he set such a good example by reading his Bible on the front porch all day every Sunday. We knew to keep Sundays a day to set apart from the others and remember the Lord. Daddy comforted me by telling me that we could trust God. He said that I was proof God did not make mistakes because God had sent me to help him and do great things with my life. Thankfully, Daddy knew to turn to the Bible during dark times. I like to think that because I looked so much like Mama, I somehow made Daddy feel close to her. I understood this much better later on in life with my own children.

My father's reputation is something all of his children, grandchildren and future generations of Hamilton descendants can be proud of. He wanted the best for us and was an example of what a man who followed after God's heart was. He always credited my mother with making him complete and getting through each day by seeing her in each one of us. I am so grateful that he said these words out loud, to us. My father never remarried which was something I did not really understand until later in life when I was standing in shoes like his.

My father had a heart attack and died at the age of 71; he lived 30 more years after Mama died. He was retired, by then, and had been to the farmers' market to buy vegetables. He ate dinner with my brother Leon and his family one evening, and they had all moved out to the front porch after dinner. Daddy said he was not feeling well, so he went back inside to lie down on the couch. As soon as Leon found him, he took him to the hospital, but it was too late.

I started to school in the fall of 1949. From what my brothers and sisters have told me, I had a very hard time adjusting to going to school every day. I was so excited to finally get on the bus and ride with them to school each morning, but once we got there, I was alone. We were all in the same building, but they were older and in different classrooms. So that I could go see them when I got scared, I created reasons to get my teacher to take me to my older sister Lena. I still remember Lena's crystal blue eyes focused on me as the door opened, and the teacher would let me walk to her desk. I whispered, "Can I have a nickel?"

Lena always gave me the same answer to this same question: "No, you cannot have a nickel because I do not have a nickel. Now go back to your class and do your schoolwork. Not much longer, and we will all go home."

I was really too young to start school, but because I was the youngest of seven children who all got up and went to school every day, I was allowed to attend. The school is still so big in my mind. Walnut School was dark green with white trim. Mrs. Ward, a teacher there, took me under her wings just like an angel. She found out that my mother was in heaven, and she wanted me to feel the love and attention I was missing.

God must have placed me on her heart. She helped me with my homework and made sure that I understood my lessons. I was very fond of Mrs. Ward and became attached to her since my father worked a lot, and my siblings and I had so many responsibilities. I am so thankful for this teacher and hope she knew how much she helped me. I am so thankful to have had my brothers and sisters, too. We were a close family, but I always missed my mother. When I was having a good day, I wished for her to be there so I could share my stories, and on a bad day, I imagined that she would hug or kiss me to let me know it was all okay.

My school years flew by, and I soon found myself in high school. Most of my brothers and sisters had already been long gone before I walked across that stage to receive my diploma. My brother Leon and I were the last two in the house. I remember Leon and me sitting with Daddy at night watching Little House on the Prairie, Gun Smoke or anything with John Wayne. In high school I thought often of what I wanted to do with my life. What I did know was that I wanted to be a wife and mother, and to serve God in the best way I could—just what every girl in the South wanted to be. My father had raised us right, and I grew up knowing that Mama was looking down on me from heaven. I liked the feeling that what I did made her smile.

Once I graduated, I began my journey into adulthood by getting a job as a waitress at Thompson's Restaurant owned by Mr. and Mrs. Howard Thompson. We served the freshest vegetables, the best catfish and smoked barbeque, and people from miles around were regulars. During lunch, the students from Mississippi

State came to eat. I never would have guessed that this would be the place where I would meet my future husband—a choice I made that changed the course of my life forever because I would always be searching for answers to what happened to Buddy Heflin.

CHAPTER 27
What We Know

I MARRIED BUDDY HEFLIN, BUT I do not know very much about his years growing up. I was going to spend the rest of my life finding out. I had meant my vows that day in June of 1961. My children were born and became my focus while Buddy and I were planning our lives; Buddy took a wrong step somewhere at some point and lost his way. I left him "once and for all" at the wise old age of 23 and moved to Chicago.

What I do not know is how or why Buddy disappeared. I do know that Buddy Heflin was the fourth child of two loving and hard-working parents. His father owned a Phillips 66 in Starkville, and Mrs. Heflin worked along-side her husband when the children were old enough to go about their own way. This family lived in a supportive and tight-knit community where they went to church and valued wholesome family life. Buddy began walking to his dad's station and eventually working at his father's business after school as soon as he was old enough. Buddy was the only son with three older sisters. It does not take too much imagination to know that he was adored and most probably spoiled rotten. Buddy was not negatively affected by all of the attention though. He got his nickname because he was so personable and friendly. He respected his parents and his teachers and the law; Buddy taught his best friend how to drive. Gail Wofford is still alive to attest to his friendship and protective nature. Buddy Heflin knew the difference between right and wrong.

Buddy Heflin was a loved little boy who grew up to be a young man who liked to fish and hunt and drive nice cars. He loved football and wanted to play on his high school team, but there his mother drew the line because she was afraid he would get hurt. Buddy continued to love football but never played himself. He graduated from high school and took a few classes at Mississippi State University. He was ambitious and when he started a family of his own, he wanted to provide for his wife and children.

The wrong step happened somewhere between graduating from high school and disappearing forever. I believe he was lured in by men who ran legitimate businesses like Kroger Grocery when behind the scenes the real money was in illegal activity. The young men like Buddy Heflin took one step too many, and it was too late when they realized the door that closed behind them could not be unlocked. The only choice for a young man who cared for those he loved was to continue walking forward into the darkness or to directly confront the men in charge who promised a swift end to anyone daring enough to defy them.

I believe the cold-blooded killers underestimated the wholesome values of Buddy Heflin and felt compelled to make an example of him. The swampy underworld that thrived in the Deep South in the 1960s wanted money so that they could gain power so that they could obtain respect and by so doing, make more money. Much of the early history of organized crime is largely inseparable from political corruption. In the early 20th century, the law had often been obliged to turn a blind eye to illegal activity because of personal investment, threat of retaliation, or political pressure. The very definition of crime that is organized is "a continuing, profit-motivated criminal enterprise that employs the use of fear, violence, intimidation, and public corruption to achieve goals and remain immune from law enforcement."

The overriding fact in my search for answers is that his car was found with bullet holes and blood, police officers promised to follow leads and investigate his disappearance, but the truth is that time was allowed to move on without any real effort to pursue where he was or what had happened.

This theory of what happened to Buddy Heflin shows Lady Justice removing the blindfold only to pretend not to see, or to actually see but look the other way as corruption, avarice, prejudice and personal gain took precedence over what is right. Lady Justice is personified as being blind to anything other than what is just in the eyes of the law. This theory has Buddy Heflin faced with one option; he would not jeopardize the safety of his mother and father, his wife and two sons, his best friends or anyone else who may have been threatened by good old boys turned cold-blooded killers.

Part V:

Photos

Alexis Heflin

Buddy Heflin National Guard

Alexis Heflin Wedding Photo

Johnny Heflin

Ricky Heflin

Alexis Heflin's siblings. Older sisters Lena (l) and Marige (r).
Older brothers (l to r) Gene, Ray, Willie F. Baby is Leon.

Alexis Heflin's Mother and Father
Callie and Cas Hamilton

Buddy Heflin (2nd from left) with sisters and friends

Buddy Heflin's Mother and Father
Ike and Sarah Heflin

Alexis Heflin

Afterword
by Valerie Leary

This story chronicles what Alexis Heflin lived with the hope that what happened to Buddy Heflin will finally surface from the depths of a metaphorical Mississippi swamp. The evidence from all reports from those closest to Buddy immediately before he vanished suggests that he had been murdered and that his body was thrown into the Mississippi River. His wife has been speculating about what happened to him for over forty years. His body has never been found, but she would like to have a grave marker made for him and placed next to his father Ike Heflin in the cemetery in Starkville.

As much as possible I write the story as told by my aunt in chronological order. What little anyone does know about Buddy Heflin's mysterious disappearance has come to light here and there over the past forty years. My aunt and I talk on a daily basis, and the focus of our conversations these past three years has been the story of her life as a result of her husband's disappearance. Logically, there is a beginning and an end to someone's life with details along the way. Emotionally, however, the paths one takes move forward, backward, sideways and at times, they stand still. New information surfaces only to lead to a dead end. More evidence surfaces from years earlier, and then it, too, leads to another dead end. In this way chronological order seemed impossible, but I resolved to write the story so that the facts of my aunt's life read like evidence in an investigation.

Moreover, the investigation is on-going. The Mississippi Bureau of Investigations is working to help those who knew Buddy to finally get the dates, evidence, statements, documents and suspicions to make sense and be logical.

That has only been in process since April of 2013 when Aunt Lexi and I drove to Starkville to meet with the agents in person to try and figure out who was in fact working on the case.

Raymond Delk the Deputy Director of the MBI was the one who had reopened the case in 2010 and had Buddy's mysterious disappearance on the fast track to a Grand Jury proceeding. I was not with my aunt at the meeting in 2010. I do know that when she returned from Mississippi, she was expecting to hear from Raymond Delk within months. Sadly, those months turned in to three years, Delk retired without a word to my aunt, and the Grand Jury hearing faded away. My aunt was waiting to hear when she should return to Mississippi for the hearing, and time began to pass by without any news at all. After repeated phone calls with no response from Raymond Delk, my aunt was finally informed that he had retired from his position with the Department of Public Safety a short time after her visit in 2010. He did not contact my aunt but left without informing her that Buddy's case was to return to a file drawer.

The drive to Starkville in April of 2013 was a game changer. She is now convinced that she has the best men whom she can trust to do their jobs with integrity. The meeting got off to a rough start because of me. I lost my temper with one of the agents within the first fifteen minutes of the interview. All was well in the end, and we left on good terms with handshakes and even hugs. We laugh now because it is all too clear why there was such a huge misunderstanding. I am a high school Language Arts teacher. I have over twenty years of experience and a reputation for keeping my classes under control. I tend not to back down too easily and to be the one who must appear cool under pressure and have the last word. The fact is that I was very nervous about meeting with the FBI. The timeline I prepared last minute for the meeting insinuated that one of the detectives had misled my aunt on purpose, and I mentioned his first name "Clay" because that was all I knew. That detective happened to be sitting in the office that morning, and he noticed his name immediately. When he questioned me with indignation about the accuracy of the timeline and my intentions for accusing him of having a poor work ethic, my anger and suspicions unleashed. The experienced federal agent and the quick-tempered English teacher had a heated debate about what exactly was documented on that time line which quickly escalated to loud voices and angry stares. Having no idea that Alexis Heflin and I were related, "Clay" suspected that I was a biased and trouble-making reporter, so when he demanded, "Who are you?" I naturally thought he was being condescending and exploded, "Who are you?" The battle for power continued while the other two agents and my aunt sat still and looked back and forth at one another until time to intervene and calm us down.

Aunt Lexi knows me well enough to know that I was being protective of her, and the older agents knew their partner well enough to know that he would never have misled my aunt or in any way undermined the responsibility of his job. He had proven himself to be reliable, trustworthy and extremely dedicated to his job of protecting and fighting for justice.

The misunderstanding was resolved, and after apologies and acknowledgments from both of us about what had *just happened, we proceeded with what turned out to be a three-hour meeting. My aunt has been in constant contact with Alan Thompson who is handling one part of the investigation. He returns her phone calls and is pursuing every lead that had been dropped in the past. The three of them are answers to her prayers. She had been looking for someone brave enough to follow through with their promises since 1970. She does not have to look further. My aunt is so grateful to these men who truly deserve the trust that people have in our law enforcement officers.*

I have learned about an organization that offers help and support to families like my aunt's family who have lost a loved one who simply vanished. The National Missing and Unidentified Persons System (NamUs) keeps records of deceased people who have been "unclaimed." The name and identity of some of these people is known, but no family member has come forward to identify the body for burial. In other cases, the bodies wait to be named and identified by someone willing to come looking for them.

REWARD

If you have information pertaining to the disappearance of Buddy Heflin, please contact:

Alan Thompson, Supervisory Special Agent
Mississippi Bureau of Investigation
22,000-A HWY 35 North
Batesville, MS 38606

ACKNOWLEDGMENTS

I would like to express my gratitude to all of you who have supported me and encouraged me to write this book.   I would specifically like to thank the following people by name:

Ann Allen

Jeff Blankenship

Allen and Melissa Brinkley

Chuck Brasher

Mike Colbert

Erica Crawford

Julie Draper

Stephanie Emerson

Ashley Evett

Tom Feltenstein

Stacy Griffis

Linda Hall

Steve Hammer

Darden Heritage

Deborah Herman

Gerald Higdon

Sandra Harris

Robert Howard

Alexis Heflin

A special acknowledgment and thanks to **Teresa Leary McLendon,** my niece, whose devotion, dedication and diligence in seeing this book through, from the beginning to the end, have been inspiring and endearing.

Lonnie Miller

Dawn Osborn

Mary Osborne

Doug Owens

Andrea Parker

Carol Potts

William Sisco

Sandra Taylor

Drew and Lane Tutt

Jessica Wingate

CPSIA information can be obtained at www.ICGtesting.com
Printed in the USA
LVOW06s1150110514

385165LV00001B/3/P